Comfortable Being Ignorant
While Surviving The Journey

JoAnn F. Cash

Dedicated To My Mother

Mrs. Evora "Doll" Fletcher

Acknowledgements

To my family whose level of hurt matched mine.
and
To my friends who went to prison with me:

Annie Ficklin
Terence Hatcher
Phyl Macon
Rosetta Mindingall
Camellia Moore
Shelia Moore
Marion Moses
Martha Robinson
Gloria Spaulding
Helen Stewart

And to all those individuals who wrote the judge
and prayed...

Thanks and God Bless

In Appreciation

*I sincerely thank the following individuals for their support in
editing this story
and assuring me that it was worth sharing with others:*

Annette Chinn
Leon Ferguson
Natalie Ferguson
Annie Ficklin
Bea Flippen
Pauline Baker-Ford
Aundra Green
Terence Hatcher
Mamie Johnson

*And a special thank you to Patricia "Trish" Lewis
who would not allow me to quit.*

Special Dedication

to

All of the children who are moving through

life in pain

and

To the mothers who are away...

Testimonials

P-H-E-N-O-M-E-N-A-L WOMAN

I have known JoAnn for what sometimes seems like forever. For the sake of brevity, I will focus my attention on the last 355 days since her release. And even so, this is but a fraction of it all. I am continually amazed, and if the truth were known, humbly stand in awe of what she has accomplished. Her vision of a Women's Summit grew from one to six with the seventh scheduled for January 2002. She wanted to address the brokenness that women of all ages face and let each know they could live healthy and whole...through Him. Lives were touched and changed.

She worked with the teens of her Church on an intense reality-based 8-week sexual abstinence program. Lives were touched and changed. She developed and executed a Girls Rites of Passage Program for the younger girls of her Church. It culminated in a Ceremony of Celibacy and each received a ring, which is worn with pride. Lives were touched and changed.

She went to work in a low-income community and was instrumental in bringing a nationally recognized childcare assistance program into the community. Others had tried and failed year after year. Lives were touched and changed.

She has worked on this book and lived out the old adage "a labor of love" and made it a reality. Lives will be touched and changed. She is without a doubt a child of the King and by anyone's standards – a P-H-E-N-O-M-E-N-A-L WOMAN.

~ Phyl R. Macon ~

Once upon a time, I met a lady, JoAnn Cash, who interviewed me for a position in her company. During the interview she looked me straight in my eyes and expressed herself and her expectations and asked if I would have any problems doing what was required. She is direct to the point, bold, out spoken, focused with a purpose and loving. She is stylish and versatile, firm but flexible and if she doesn't know something, she will take the time to learn. I am very impressed with who God created her to be...

~ Caroline Taylor, a Friend Indeed ~

JoAnn Cash A Faithful Servant

I was invited to Metro Transitional Center on December 3, 2000 by one of the chaplains to tour the center and to meet JoAnn Cash in person. It was Advent Sunday and while the Chaplain was preparing for the evening service, she asked me if I wanted to go into the classroom where a group of ladies were gathered together expressing their well wishes to JoAnn who would be leaving the center the next day.

I sat there mesmerized and was totally blown away at all the accolades and love that was bestowed upon this woman. When the session was over, I introduced myself to JoAnn and we were allowed to visit privately in the "Blue Room." Our spirits connected immediately and by the time our visit had ended, it was quite obvious that God had allowed JoAnn to be sent to prison not for a crime she did not commit, but as an assignment for Him. As you read her reenactment of 1,032 days of incarceration, you will see that JoAnn demonstrated that same faith as "Job" and truly trusted God for everything. I am grateful that God has allowed this woman to come into my life and I am proud to call her my friend..

~ P.A. Trish Lewis ~
Executive Director, SA'Mira's Place, Inc.

JoAnn Cash has been an active member of the First Corinth Missionary Baptist Church for many years serving in various positions as a leader and friend to fellow Christians. Over the years, her love for others and admiration for the church has been shared through her work and good deeds within the church, the community and wherever there was a need. The lives of many youth, parents, men and women have been blessed through seminars, workshops, group sessions and programs designed to help the participants be better individuals in our society.

Many times when people are faced with adversity or are being tested, they give up and seem to forget who is in control. There are others who become stronger and their faith in God is more evident. During the past year Mrs. Cash has shown a spiritual growth and a greater desire to serve. She is a living testimony to others about what God can do and is doing in her life. To God be the Glory and may you forever be blessed.

~ Rev. E.L. Jones, Pastor ~
First Corinth Missionary Baptist Church

I met JoAnn Fletcher Cash fifteen years ago when I was a case manager for Fulton DFCS and her agency was a contract service provider for Fulton County Department of Family and Children Services.

JoAnn advocated for children and parents and provided case management support for me. She attended juvenile court hearings and interceded on behalf of families. Her parenting groups and family counseling sessions were effective.

It is a privilege and a pleasure to have developed this professional relationship with JoAnn. She is a jewel for families, womanhood and sisterhood.

~ Pauline Baker-Ford ~

Forward

To say JoAnn is unique would not be description enough. To say she is extraordinary would only scratch the surface. But to say she is a woman of great substance, a woman of prayer and a woman of immense faith, would begin to define this unbelievable person.

JoAnn has been my friend since 1972 and I have been blessed to be a participant observer in the metamorphosis that has occurred in her life. It is impossible to be her friend and not to have had some type hands-on involvement in her many exploits into advocating change in the lives of those persons who lack the means to advocate for themselves. This calling to advocate has produced the material that is the basis of this novel.

That JoAnn has the will to recall the trauma that has existed in her life the past four-five years, by reliving the details so passionately in this novel, is a testament to her faith and strength. I know that after you have read the very chilling recounting of what happened to my friend, the only conclusion that can be drawn is that, but for the grace of God something similar could happen to you!

I am convinced that God has a chosen role for each of us to play on this stage of life, and further convinced that JoAnn was chosen for this. I admire her strength and thank God for the way her life has touched mine.

Rosetta Torbert Mindingall

Introduction

For many years, family and friends asked me, why don't you write a book? I would ask, a book about what? They replied, a book about you and your life. You just don't know how different you are.

At times I would get a bit upset and offended by that remark, asking what they meant? There are no two individuals alike! So what is so different about me that several people would ask me about writing an autobiography?

One evening, as my husband, Calvin, and I sat on our patio, he jokingly said to me, JoAnn, you need to write a book! I got really mad at him, because, by now, I was a little fed up with hearing that remark. And I responded, why should "I" write a book, I'm no freak! I simply could not see what there was about me to write a book about.

Calvin tried to tell me that I was not a freak, but unique. He said that throughout our twenty plus years of marriage, he had seen me involved in situations that typically did not happen. And he felt that some of the incidents were worth sharing with others, even though he did not go into details or give specific examples.

Several months after that conversation, James Browne, a gentleman who owned a publishing company, asked me about writing a book. at the time, he was involved with some independent contracting work with my agency. He also told me that I was very interesting and unique. James said that I should consider taking a leave of absence from my job with the school system to write this book. He said, "all you need is time".

Well, with all of this previous encouragement, one might ask, "why now" when in the past I refused to respond. But the circumstances have changed. The difference is that while previously I did not have it, I do now. I do have time. Two days ago I was convicted of a crime, which by the way, I did not commit, and I am being held in jail, without bond. So you see, I do have time.

There was nothing extremely unusual occurring in my life leading up to these occurrences, other than life was going well. Many times I would find myself thanking GOD for HIS goodness. And telling HIM that if I'm too high, please bring me down. I was not afraid to pray that prayer because we had a very long-term relationship. I trusted HIM and I knew that whatever HE did, it was for my good.

Contents

Chapter 1

WHEN YOU HAVE BEEN CHOSEN

I was at home frying chicken, when the telephone rang. It was South Fulton Hospital calling me as legal guardian for Ms. Addie Beddington. She had a heart attack and had been admitted. They wanted me, as her legal guardian, to come to the hospital to take care of the necessary paperwork for her admission.

Ms. Beddington, who was Caucasian, and I had a very unique relationship. Her grandson, James Peacock, had been one of the first students I had placed on my caseload back in 1976 when I went to work for the school system. James was in a special program (first grade) for children who had severe behavior problems. And Ms. Beddington relied on my advice to make decisions concerning his schooling.

James remained in school until high school, but had extensive involvement with the juvenile court. He grew up and was sent off to prison but Ms. Beddington and I continued our relationship. After her husband died, she decided to appoint me as her legal guardian to assist her in her business matters. My name was placed on all of her important papers and that was the reason the hospital called me.

That phone call was the last thing I needed in my life. I was already overwhelmed. I was trying to raise my ten year old son, be a wife, work full time, as a social worker with a local school system, emotionally support my older sister, Jannette Fletcher, we affectionately call her "Pumpkin" who has multiple sclerosis and had just stopped walking, maintain telephone contact with Mr. and Mrs. Edward Parrish about mother, who was in the hospital in Brunswick. Her doctors were trying to decide whether or not she needed to have open-heart surgery.

Needless to say, I was stressed out. I immediately went to the hospital and took care of the necessary paperwork. After sitting in the emergency room for more than eight hours, waiting to hear if Ms. Beddington would live or die, I felt at the end of my rope. It was almost 3:00 o'clock in the morning and I was dog-tired. I knew that I had to get up around 6:30 to get my son up for breakfast and ready for school and myself ready for work.

While sitting in that emergency room I asked God to please keep me from going crazy. I asked Him to take some of the pressure off me and if He was not willing to do that, to please, please put something else on my mind. I was sick and tired of worrying all the time.

The moment I prayed that prayer, a voice said, "well open a counseling center." I immediately looked around to see who spoke to me and no one was there. I was alone in the emergency room. I looked at the clock and it was 2:40 a.m.

About 3:30 a.m. Ms. Beddington was discharged from the hospital to follow up with her doctor on the following Monday (This all started on a Thursday evening). I had her prescriptions filled for her medication and took her home and made sure that she got into bed.

That voice nagged me all weekend long. I never really thought about opening any kind of business...but then I started to think about possible locations. I just felt that, if I would consider opening an office, it should be somewhere in South Fulton County, (East Point or College Park) or South Atlanta (Campbellton Road or Cleveland Avenue), because resources for African Americans were limited.

The following Monday, I took Ms. Beddington to the doctor for her follow-up appointment. When we arrived at the doctor's office, it was crowded with no available seats in the waiting area. The staff took Ms. Beddington on "in the back" to wait for the doctor. I told her that I had a little errand to run and would be back to pick her up by the time the doctor had finished with her.

Her doctor's office was located just off Cleveland Avenue. I rode down Cleveland Avenue trying to figure out how to go about finding an office. I looked at several realty signs while riding down Cleveland Avenue until I came to a building and noticed a sign that read Frank Middlebrooks Realty Company.

While attending college at Albany State College, (University, now) there was a Frank Middlebrooks enrolled there but I had not seen him in almost twenty years. I decided to stop at that company and ask someone if they could help me locate office space. This whole thing was kind of outrageous for me because I had absolutely no money.

As I started up the stairs leading to Frank Middlebrooks Realty, the door opened and down the steps walked Frank Middlebrooks from Albany State College. After we greeted each other, he turned around and took me back to his office and we sat down to talk. I told him that I needed some help locating office space and I did not have any funds available to do so. Then he asked me several questions like, what hours I needed the space, and I told him late afternoon because I was employed with a local school system, full time. We discussed how many days of the week the office would be needed and how much rent I could afford. I told him maybe three evenings a week and he told me to just pay what I could afford towards rent.

I talked to my closest friend, Rosetta Mindingall, about coming into partnership with me. She was employed with the juvenile court and had very good counseling skills (especially with me) and excellent credentials. At first she was hesitant because she had dreamed of opening a "special needs" day care center. But after some mild arm-twisting, she agreed to become my partner. And she came up with the name for the agency – Hand-in-Hand Counseling Service.

My first client was Michelle Smith, daughter of a very good friend of mine. I made a copy of her check for $60.00 per hour; she paid to talk to me. Referrals were rather slow in coming but suddenly Frank's real estate business started to grow and his agents began working in his office late evenings and at night. I knew pretty soon that we would have to find some place else for office space.

About two weeks after realizing that we needed to move (I was not going to wait until Frank had to ask us to), I was sitting on my front porch . . . kind of talking to God about where do I go from here? At that time my next-door neighbor, Michael Babb, and his brother, Errol drove up.

Errol and Michael were disappointed that I had not attended their wives' open house of their beauty salon the previous week. I told them about my dilemma of needing some office space... with no funds available.

Michael suggested to Errol that maybe they could help. Their wives' beauty salon was located in an old house on Lakewood Avenue that Michael and Errol had renovated into a beautiful site. The other half of the house was also the location of their new office... Christian Brothers Construction Company. They were thinking that, with little or no effort, they could renovate their attic for office space for me.

I met them at their location the following day and they had decided to allow me to use two of the offices located in Christian Brothers Construction Company. The rent was to be whatever Rosetta and I could afford. God had again "made a way"

We had a few more referrals and remained in that office for approximately four months. However that location was less than ideal because at night (which was when we saw our clients because I was still working full time at South Metro (school system) and Rosetta with the juvenile court, it was scary entering and leaving the building. Also the area was less than desirable for our clients who often had to ride public transportation and walk a little distance to and from the office.

It was while we were on Lakewood Avenue that one of my longtime (dating back to college) friends, Maxine Grimes, informed me that Lennie Wilson was very interested in becoming a part of the agency. I knew of Lennie and felt comfortable with her because of her reputation working with the Head Start Program and her credentials were good. After some discussion with Rosetta, we agreed to allow Lennie to become a part of the organization.

During August of 1988, we all started to look for some affordable office space. Instead of relying on word-of-mouth referrals (because we had no funds for advertising) we considered submitting a bid to contract to provide counseling for the juvenile court. Rosetta insisted that she drop out of the business to avoid a conflict of interest because she was employed full time with the juvenile court. And to contract with the juvenile court was an excellent opportunity for the agency.

Lennie and I decided to concentrate our search for office space to the East Point and College Park area because, other than Families First, there were very few resources available in South Fulton County. And to my knowledge, there were none that targeted African American families. We first looked at The Buggy Works Building off Cleveland Avenue and then went to look at Harrison Square on Old National Highway in College Park.

Prior to going to look for office space of our own, which was nothing but an act of faith because Lennie was pretty much like me (low on funds),

I had a dream. In the dream, I envisioned a building that sat in the center of other buildings. In our particular office, there was a reception area and several offices, each providing quality counseling that was empowering families and individuals to reach their fullest potential. I was very proud of what I saw the agency doing but more important than me, God was pleased.

Old National Highway

While I had traveled up and down Old National Highway for years, I had never entered the Harrison Square Office complex. It was the nicest looking office property in the area.

In January 1989, Lennie and I met at Harrison Square to look at office space. Once I turned into the complex, I knew it was the right location because the building that sat in the center of the complex facing Old National Highway was the very same building I had seen in my dream.

We met with the leasing manager and looked at some offices in the building behind the big building in the center. Whatever the big building's rent was, I never asked, because I felt sure that it was totally out of the question for us at that time.

The site we decided upon would rent for $1,000.00 per month with a minimum of a three years lease. That amounted to a $36,000.00 commitment. Lennie suggested that we each come up with $2,500.00 for our first month's rent, deposit and office furnishings. She had just recuperated from a traffic accident and was expecting a large financial settlement. So there were no problems with her getting her $2500.00. And me, I had nothing and nobody.

I was just returning to work from Christmas holidays and felt that everyone that I knew was as broke as I was . . . except Johnny West, father of my first client, Michelle. His son Danny was on my caseload at school and his wife, Sue, (Danny's step-mother), and I had somehow become friends. I say somehow, because I usually made it a point to never have a personal relationship with any of "my parents" from school. All contacts were strictly professional. I don't know when it happened but Sue and I crossed the line. Our relationship was not one of parent-social worker, but instead . . . very close friends. We were more like sisters, she White, me, Black.

While washing dishes one Saturday morning, I was talking to God . . . asking Him to please show me what to do. And I wanted Him to tell me just how you ask someone to loan you $2,500.00. I knew Johnny West had it (because he was rich) but his wife, my friend, was a homemaker and had no income.

While trying to figure out what to do, the telephone rang. It was Sue West calling. I told her that I was, at that very moment, thinking about how to ask her husband to loan me $2,500.00 so that we could move our office. Sue said that was a bad idea to ask her husband because he did not loan money. He stopped loaning money years ago. Sue then said she would be glad to give the money to me because she was happy to help me help others. She also said that I had no idea just how good a counselor I really was. Sue said she would like to see the office space, if possible, so I scheduled to meet her at the site the following week during my lunch hour. When I arrived at Harrison Square, the day I was to meet Sue, she was parked in the parking lot waiting for me. I told her we would have to get the complex manager to open the office for her to see. She said no . . . she had thought about it and she did not need to see it. She said for me to go and help others the same way I had helped her family. And pay me back, if you want to! She then handed me twenty-five one hundred dollars bills. I broke down and cried.

A couple of days later, I met with Lennie to make our final plans for paying our deposit and securing our office space. This is when she informed me that she was not able to come up with her half of the money ($2,500.00) for us to get started.

After a lot of prayer, I met with the leasing office manager on Dr. Martin Luther King, Jr's Birthday, 1989 and paid the deposit and signed the lease for three years occupancy at $1,000.00 per month. That was truly an act of faith because I committed to paying a total of $36,000.00 in rent when I had a total of $11.36 in my checking account.

I talked with my mother and Ms. Beddington about my plans. They both wished me well. Mother reminded me that in order to be a success . . . always make God the head of my life. This was something she mentioned because by now, she felt like she should have drummed it into my head. She knew that if I would trust God, then everything would be all right.

Mother sent me a check for $100.00 that she borrowed from Mr. Parrish, to help pay for my business cards and letterhead stationary. Ms. Beddington saved $50.00 worth of pennies, wrapped them and took them to the bank. She called me to her apartment and presented me with a $50.00 bill. They were the full extent of my financial backers.

For the first month, referrals were slow. Michelle was still coming and a few phone calls were coming in. Then, once the referrals started to increase, mainly for family counseling . . . all of the clients were Caucasian.

I continued to pray . . . kind of reminding God that my reason for opening this counseling service was to provide professional counseling to African Americans. It was several months before we had our first Black clients, a little boy whose father had been killed in a freak accident on the expressway and his mother. He was really acting out in school. I was so happy to see them that their first session was "on the house."

Our referrals continued to increase. My joy came in providing the actual counseling and telling others about the agency while Lennie focused on the business aspects . . . who paid and who owed. I really disliked looking at the financial part because "it took the fun" out of it all. I began to provide services to individuals and families whether they had money to pay or not. I knew that problems did not wait until we had money!

We had our first Open House on February 24, 1989, during a less than ideal time. It was an extremely cold day, twenty-two degrees and a day that was a "teacher workday". We had been relying on school personnel to drop by after work. We had mailed invitations to juvenile court staff, the Department of Family and Children Services (DFACS) and Court Services personnel as well.

I was running a little later than planned for Open House. I had gotten a new haircut for the occasion and was having a bad case of "the nerves." I asked God to help me be able to handle the small turnout and not be disappointed.

When I arrived at the office complex, I could barely find a parking space in our area. There were well-wishers throughout each office, reception area and conference room. I was shocked because not only was Sue West there, but also with her was her husband, Johnny, who in the past made no attempt to hide his dislike for African Americans. He had tried to avoid doing business in Atlanta for ten years to keep from coming in contact with African Americans, (per his wife, Sue). There were approximately seventy individuals in attendance throughout the evening. I thanked God!

The week following open house, I received a call from Johnny West. He told me how impressed he was with the agency and the things that I was trying to do. He also thanked me for my help with his son, Danny. Johnny also told me that if I ever needed some financial assistance, please call him before I called anyone else.

That April 1989, Sue invited my son and me to spend the weekend with her and her family at their new cabin in the mountains. And I accepted the invitation. Johnny had purchased a house as a Christmas present for Sue and he bought himself an airplane. We were scheduled to leave on a Saturday morning, but the Thursday before we were to take the trip, my son, Calvin, had one of his bouts with bronchitis and had to be absent from school for two days.

The day before the trip, I was taking a nap and dreamed about an airplane crash. I saw the rescue team trying to make its way to a plane that had crashed into some trees. The telephone rang. It was Sue calling, confirming that we were still going with them (the next day), for the weekend and giving me directions to the private airstrip. I informed her of my son's illness and expressed my concerns about his breathing in a small plane. Because of his condition, I told her we would not be able to go this time and thanked her for the invitation.

Sue and Johnny West, along with Sue's oldest daughter from her previous marriage, Sue's granddaughter and Michelle flew to their cabin in the mountains. This was Johnny's first solo pilot flight in his new plane. The plane crashed on a mountaintop and every one aboard was killed except Michelle. I have dedicated my services to making Sue proud, and have hung a plaque in our office in her memory.

It was during this time that my husband, Calvin, filed the necessary paperwork and incorporated the agency through the Secretary of State's office. The agency's official name became Hand-in-Hand Counseling Services, Inc. He used his knowledge of the law to assist the agency with a lot of business matters.

Our referrals began to increase and we were offered our first contract with DFACS to provide "on-site" counseling services to youth at Oak Hill Homes. We began to hire counselors to assist us in our mission . . . to provide quality counseling to those who are sick and tired of being sick and tired.

Because the agency provided non-traditional counseling, which targeted actual behavior instead of psychological factors or traditional causes for it, I recruited certified Behavior Disorders (B.D.) teachers to work with the agency. I even "drafted" several individuals I had worked with first hand through the school system. In an effort to provide the best counseling available, our staff had to be "a cut above the rest."

Due to the quality of the services provided at Hand-in-Hand, our referrals, (through one person telling another,) continued to increase. We made the request and were awarded contracts to provide counseling services to the Juvenile Court, DFACS and Court Services. God was continuing to bless the agency beyond my wildest imagination.

Hollywood Court

In an effort to expand our services, my oldest sister, Punkin, told me of her neighbor, Dr. Rachel Muhammed, a Licensed Clinical Psychologist, who was looking for part-time employment. Punkin said they were talking about the agency and 'the doctor" was very interested in meeting with me to offer her expertise as well as to open up a new source of referrals . . . Medicaid recipients. Dr. Muhammed was currently working in nursing homes with Medicare recipients but welcomed the opportunity to work with youth. And she looked forward to serving the Medicaid population, which was grossly under-served. She stated that it was a simple matter of her filling out a few forms . . . and we would be well on our way.

During this same period, my church, First Corinth Baptist Church, adopted a public housing project . . . Hollywood Courts. As part of the services extended to that community, my pastor, Rev. Eddie L. Jones extended an invitation to Hand-in-Hand Counseling Services, Inc. to be a part of this adoption. That collaboration gave birth to the second office in Hollywood Courts Public Housing Complex.

Our Hollywood Courts office was housed in a four-bedroom town-house apartment, donated by the Atlanta Housing Authority. Although, like me, African American and primarily low-income, many of these residents seemed to have come from another planet, another culture. . with a very different value system. We were able to provide, under the supervision of Dr. Muhammed, individual, family and group counseling, tutoring, a G.E.D. Program, Parenting Program and the P.E.A.C.H. Program for mothers.

The office was very attractive, especially for the area . . . wall-to-wall carpet (donated by a community entrepreneur, Dianne Mitchell), a large palm tree in the reception area (donated by a resident, Annette Mabry) and ceiling fans in every office. And we even had carpet on our front porch. We were told initially that "outsiders" were not welcome in the area and we needed to be prepared to replace all broken windows and stolen office furnishings.

During the entire eighteen months that we were housed in that location, we did not have one broken window or one break in. And the agency empowered approximately three hundred residents of Hollywood Courts and the surrounding neighborhood.

The office was a much-needed service in the area. While the agency thoroughly enjoyed the opportunity to provide services to Medicaid recipients

... it was extremely frustrating trying to find out exactly what was expected from the agency as far as being in compliance with their rules were concerned.

Dr. Muhammed was our only link with Medicaid, having completed all of their paperwork. But she wanted to "stop by" the Hollywood Courts office in the evenings on her way home from her full time position with the county. She stated that she was "more than comfortable" with the services being provided at the Old National office because of her familiarity with the staff. Because the same staff, for the most part was being used at both offices, she saw no need to put in more time with supervision. She wanted the offices to continue to provide family, individual, group counseling and tutoring.

I discussed with Lennie what seemed like "awfully lax supervision" of the Hand-in-Hand staff by Dr. Muhammed. More than once, Lennie assured me that the Medicaid doctors (based on her professional experiences with doctors she had previously worked with through Economic Opportunity Atlanta, (E.O.A.) or mental health centers) really only wanted to be paid and did not really care about the Medicaid recipient.

Based upon many experiences I had with mental health doctors working with "my kids" in the school system, I agreed that the quality of services provided by them was not what I would have wanted for my son, Calvin. And many of the parents I worked with in the school system consistently complained about the quality of care received by their children through Medicaid.

I certainly was not impressed with the Medicaid system and began to put a lot more pressure on our staff. I constantly reminded them "we are our brother's keeper." As a staff, we had to be "a cut above the rest" to take up the slack for the doctor. Our clients would not have to settle for second best simply because it seemed that the doctor did not care.

When I approached Dr. Muhammed about the agency's compliance with Medicaid, she assured me that everything was in good shape as long as the staff followed her directions. She also reminded me that if anything was wrong, she was the provider and the one liable ... not the agency. She also stated that if there were any violations with the services we provided, her license could be in jeopardy and that was her livelihood.

Dr. Muhammed told me about the provider agreement and stated that even the check would be issued in her name and sent (for everyone's convenience) to the Hand-in-Hand address. She also told me that my name was nowhere on any papers. The liability was all hers and she knew what she was doing.

It continued to "nag" at me ... the quality of supervision provided by Dr. Muhammed. To ensure that Hand-in-Hand Counseling Services, Inc. was doing what it was supposed to ... the agency hired (part-time) Marion Carter, a Licensed Social Worker, who worked (full-time) at a mental health facility making sure that it was following Medicaid's guidelines. Her job responsibility at Hand-in-Hand was to make sure that we were in compliance with the Medicaid rules and regulations.

Lennie, Marion, and Dr. Muhammed met and developed a procedural manual that would ensure consistency at both offices. Then they met with the staff to provide them with training so that we could be in compliance with Medicaid.

After our Open House celebration for the Hollywood Courts Office, the agency was making a tremendous impact on families in Metro Atlanta and surrounding areas. And Dr. Muhammed became more involved with the staff and clients. The agency was serving a population that would, for the most part, go under-served because they did not believe in traditional therapy.

A major part of the success of the agency was the fact that we were professional, caring and committed. We offered a personal touch that could not be matched by other agencies. And we, as a staff, put God first and when needed or requested, would often pray with and for our clients. We cared and showed it!! And our clients appreciated it.

Things seemed to be going well in the Atlanta area. I had just neglected my family, trying to know what was going on in both offices and still work with the school system. By the time I got home in the late evening, I often was too tired to eat or even think. My husband and son simply carried on without me.

Many people asked why I continued to work for the school system, since the agency was doing so well. I would tell them that Hand-in Hand Counseling Services, Inc. was my mission; I did not want money for helping people. God had given me an opportunity to do it. I did not want money for what I did at the agency. I continued to work for the school system to help with my personal and family financial obligations.

Brunswick

In July 1990, I decided to get away and looked forward to a much needed rest at my mother's house in Brunswick. While sitting on her front porch in her swing (one of my favorite things to do), an agent from the Independent Life Insurance Company came to collect mother's insurance money. The lady asked me if I was Ms. Fletcher's daughter and when I answered yes, she then wanted to know if I was the one who was a school counselor in Atlanta and had opened my own counseling business up there. Yes, was the answer to that question as well.

The lady from the insurance agency then told me about her fifteen year old son who had been "put out" of school until he could receive three counseling sessions. He had attended one session with "an old white doctor" who could not relate to her son and the doctor's fee was $125.00 per hour.

The doctor's office had informed her that his schedule was booked for the month. The only way he could guarantee the mother that he could see her son two more times before school started was for her to pay twice his fee and that would move her son to the top of the waiting list.

The lady felt that she had no choice because her son was having problems in school that she felt were directly related to his dad being ill and currently unable to provide for his family. She stated that her son was simply afraid that his dad was going to die. And it was fear that was causing him to act out. Her son had no previous history of behavior problems in school.

Anyway . . . to have her son seen, because this was the only way that he could return to school in the fall, was to pay the doctor $250.00 per hour. Her son had to have two more sessions and the family was strained financially.

The insurance agent said she would find the $500.00 to pay the doctor because her son had to go to school. His non-attendance was not an option. He would be a tenth grader and she intended to attend a graduation . . . his. She also asked me if I would please open an office in Brunswick so Black children could get counseling from their own people.

That night, I again dreamed about Hand-in-Hand Counseling Services, Inc. and realized that it would grow to be a big success . . . possibly on an international scale. I envisioned a large building surrounded by several smaller buildings. They kind of reminded me of bomb shelters with a protective covering.

Before I really entertained the idea of Hand-in-Hand (Brunswick), I sought out my father figure and advisor, Mr. Edward L. Parrish, the same one who had loaned my mother the $100.00 when I first got started with the agency. His wife, Mrs. Winnie Parrish had been my mentor and role model and I credit her for my choosing the field of social services as my career. They lived directly across the street from mother and while I was in high school, she was my juvenile probation officer. But that's another story for another time.

Anyhow, I sought out Mr. Parrish, a retired school- teacher and my father figure, about the possibility of opening an office in Brunswick. After a lengthy discussion about the two offices in the Atlanta area and the services they offered (counseling and not therapy) as well as its target population (African Americans). . Mr. Parish said, "I think you just might have something here." It was not so much what he said . . . but the way he said it. And then he pledged his support for the agency. I was scared but I felt that this was what God wanted me to do.

My next step in considering Hand-in-Hand (Brunswick) was to go to my long-time friend and classmate, Gloria Spaulding, (Class of 65'). While in high school, I told Gloria and one or two others, that I had a feeling that one day, I would go to jail. I also told them that when I called, don't ask me what I did . . . just come on and get me out of jail and I would tell them all about it on our way home. And I never let Gloria forget that promise. Anyway, it was crucial for me to know whether or not the local residents would be receptive to a counseling office that targeted African-Americans and whether or not they felt there was a need for one in their area.

Gloria and I talked about some of the grass roots level individuals who were involved in the African American community. My desire was to hear from the locals and give them an opportunity to express their desire as to what services, if any, should be offered. My goal was to make sure that that office, if it was going to exist, be "tailor-made" to meet the local needs. We decided to invite some of the community people to her house and ask them about the possibilities.

Never in my wildest imagination could I have predicted the response in Brunswick.

Forty-two individuals representing a cross section of the community involved with everything from the school system to politics were in attendance. The idea of a local counseling service geared towards meeting the needs of African American families was very well received. And Gloria's sister-in-law, Alberta Spaulding, catered nothing short of a "seafood feast" for the occasion, serving every kind of seafood imaginable. I thanked God for what He had done!

Once it was established that the area was receptive to a Hand-in-Hand, Brunswick, I again sought out Mr. Parrish and a long time school friend, Jewell Clark, to locate office space. I told them that I would like a place that was centrally located and that could be used to meet the needs of "at-risk" families, regardless of color.

A couple of weeks after our initial conversation, Jewell called and informed me that she had located a possible site. I asked her to have Mr. Parrish look at it first. After visiting the site, Mr. Parrish felt that it would be a good location especially since it was located in the central part of town where 'at-risk' families lived and right next door to the Department of Family and Children Services.

I went to Brunswick to look at the office space, along with Jewell and Gloria. When I saw it, there was a special "anointing" present ... and I just knew that it was the right place, and that God was continuing to bless me. As I was leaving the office space that morning, I was simply overwhelmed by the goodness of God and I collapsed in the corner of the hallway and cried like a baby.

We recruited some of Brunswick's finest in the field of social services and education to become a part of the local staff. They were eager to rise to the challenge of meeting the needs of "at-risk" families. And we celebrated our open house on December 28, 1990.

Overall the turnout for open house was small due to the lack of advertisement. However, present were Mr. Clint Atwater, Assistant Secretary of State, who was in town on other business and Rev. E.C. Tillman, a very popular, and powerful local State Representative and Pastor of my home church, Shiloh Baptist Church. He also married my husband and I back in June of 1971. A television station and a local newspaper also covered the open house. The affair was also attended by about ten of the staff from the Atlanta office.

Initially, the Brunswick office operated on a sliding fee scale and also was blessed with a contract to provide counseling for the Glynn County Department of Family and Children Services. The office provided individual, family, marriage and couples/relationship counseling to families in the area. And several of the clients were Caucasian as well.

Several of the Brunswick office staff began to question what was in place to serve the Medicaid recipient. Dr. Muhammed said she could complete the necessary paperwork, the same as she had done for the Old National and Hollywood Courts offices so that the Medicaid population in Brunswick could be served as well.

Although I was less than satisfied with the quality of Dr. Muhammed's supervision in the Atlanta offices, I was willing to provide the services (Medicaid) in Brunswick because Marion Carter had been hired to go to Brunswick as well. Her assignment was to make sure that everything done in that office was in compliance with Medicaid, the same as she had done with the Atlanta offices. Her full time position required her to assure Medicaid compliance in a local mental health center. Consequently, she was hired, part-time, to provide the same services for our agency at each of our offices.

My desire for the Brunswick office was the same as for the two Atlanta offices. I was committed to meeting the needs of African Americans, specifically, by offering services from their own kind, an African American doctor. I conducted a thorough search, including reviewing the statewide printout from the Secretary of State's office, of all Georgia licensed psychologist, for a licensed psychologist in the Brunswick area. Based on my findings, the closest licensed African-American psychologist lived in Savannah, GA. And the ones contacted were not available.

Shortly after advertising with several statewide professional organizations for assistance in locating an African American Medicaid provider for our Brunswick office, I received a phone call from a childhood friend and former next door neighbor, Joyce Brown. She had separated from her husband and moved back to Brunswick with her children.

Joyce told me of the excessive abuse she had endured from her husband. As a result of watching this abuse, she feared that her sons had lost respect for her as their mother. Her children were experiencing difficulties, especially at school, and she desperately wanted some counseling for them. As a result of her request, Joyce Brown's sons were the first Medicaid recipients to receive counseling services in the Brunswick office.

Once the Brunswick office began flourishing with Medicaid clients, Dr. Muhammed's performance became increasingly unsatisfactory. It was during this time that she requested that her husband, who had very limited credentials, be hired as a part of the Hand-in-Hand staff. She also expressed her desire to be paid more than the twenty percent of the gross income that she was currently receiving and be allowed to hire counseling staff, including her husband.

Dr. Muhammed and I were unable to reach an admirable agreement about her receiving more money and her hiring staff. Those issues compounded with the fact that, with her new promotion, she would be having more responsibilities on her full time job. And she had a new baby. She terminated her employment with the agency. However, because she was impressed and believed in the services Hand-in-Hand were providing, she recommended Dr. Rosaland White to work with supervising the staff so that we could continue to serve the Medicaid recipients.

Once Dr. White was interviewed and a verbal agreement was reached, it included the supervision of the Brunswick staff as well as monitoring the client's files and providing feedback to the staff at all three locations.

Because the staff lacked adequate supervision in the past, the client's files were not properly documented with the appropriate terminology. After viewing the files, Dr. White discontinued the tutoring sessions and instructed staff, under the supervision of Maxine Grimes, to rewrite some of the client's notes so that they would be in compliance with Medicaid. She and one of her associates visited the Brunswick office to complete psychological evaluations on each client.

Dr. White felt that all clients involved in the agency needed a psychological evaluation to assist her in making her diagnosis. She also provided psychological evaluations for the clients from our Old National and Hollywood Courts offices as well. These evaluations were completed at her office in College Park. The trips to the doctor's office to have the psychological evaluations completed were the beginning of the agency's involvement with non-emergency transportation because Medicaid also paid to have their clients transported to appointments.

Overall, I felt more secure with the supervision provided by Dr. White. She provided staff training and seemed to care about the clients and our staff. And she expressed her admiration for the services being provided. Also she agreed to assist us in our efforts to locate an African American, licensed clinical psychologist for the Brunswick area. That would ensure more consistent and direct supervision to that staff.

Dr. White requested that Medicaid make Hand-in-Hand Counseling Services, Inc. the payee so that she would not have to be responsible for all of the income at tax time. She was involved with the agency as an independent consultant. It was agreed that she would receive twenty percent of the weekly gross for supervision of the staff at all three locations. However, she would be compensated separately for any and all psychological evaluations completed by her or her staff.

Dr. White would bill Medicaid directly for the psychological evaluations. She also designated two days a week for billing instead of the dates of service so that it would not conflict with the billing dates at her office. It was from her that I learned that I no longer needed to pay several hundred dollars a month to a local, private cab company to transport our clients to the Brunswick office for their appointments. They were eligible for non-emergency transportation and Medicaid paid for that service as well.

One African American psychologist in the area was located at Kings Bay Naval Air Station, just outside of Brunswick, Dr. William Hamilton. He was only a partial answer to my dilemma because, while he was willing to provide supervision to the staff, he was not associated with Medicaid. He was not one of their doctors because he was not licensed in Georgia, having missed passing the test by two points.

A presentation was made to Mr. Clint Atwater, Assistant Secretary of State, on behalf of the agency in an effort to help us make sure that we were in compliance with Medicaid as well as help Dr. Hamilton become licensed. Mr. Atwater made several phone calls for us after our presentation, but ultimately he was unable to give us any assistance. He did state that he knew that the entire Medicaid Policy was ambivalent.

I guess by now that one would wonder why I just did not contact Medicaid myself to get a copy of their guidelines. Well, I made numerous attempts to call the Department of Medical Assistance, (D.M.A.), the agency responsible for the supervision of Medicaid, to ask for clarification. Even when asking for the name of a specific individual, the D.M.A. would ask me for my provider number. When I told them I did not have a provider number but had one of their providers on my staff, no one at the D.M.A. would accept my calls.

Once, a representative of Medicaid returned a call Anne Simpson, the coordinator for the Atlanta office made to them on behalf of our agency. But she was out of the office when the call was returned. Anne made several attempts to reach the individual but failed. So . . . I was in the position of having to rely on the feedback given to me by their providers.

There was a tremendous move of God occurring in the three offices at the same time. Families were being empowered, self-esteem was being increased and broken hearts were being mended. Overall the agency was working to improve the quality of life for all of the individuals involved ... including the staff.

It was during this time that Satan raised his ugly head to remind me that he was still alive and well. One Sunday night as I sat on my bed, my son got out of the shower and came and sat down on my bed beside me. He told me that he had to talk to me about something and make me understand why he had to do it. Calvin and I have always been able to talk to each other about anything.

Calvin informed me that the following day, during his lunch hour at school, he was to be "beat-down" and initiated into the Crypts gang. He told me that it was necessary because he did not have sisters and brothers to help him fight if he was "jumped" by more than one individual, which is how most boys fight nowadays. He was not a fighter but was thinking ahead, trying to be in a position to defend himself if need be.

Needless to say, I was devastated . . . just the idea of my son being in a gang. I told him that I realized that he was having a hard time with my household rules and his curfew but it was because other parents did not take parenting as seriously as I did. Working with children everyday, I saw, first hand, the results of ineffective parenting.

I told Calvin that I would organize a group at Hand-in-Hand, with boys like him . . . who had rules and regulations at home that they knew they had to follow. He told me that "groups" do not fight for you, gang members do. This lead to the organization of the agency's Mentoring Program. After writing a twelve-week curriculum designated to empower, motivate, enhance, and enrich, a selected group of adolescents were paid a stipend to be trained to represent the agency.

The group became involved in weekend outdoor retreats, church sponsored skating parties, church over night lock-ins, and youth day programs. Before I knew it, girls were inquiring about a group for them as well. As a result, the agency organized a group, which consisted of a total of sixty-two male and female adolescents.

Several of the agency's mentors from the Atlanta office traveled to Brunswick and helped the Brunswick mentors with their participation in a youth day program held at Gloria's church. These young people came from all over the metro Atlanta area, and Brunswick and were representative of our future leadership. And they, along with my son, made me proud!

While the agency was offering a much-needed service at the Hollywood Courts office, Satan became involved by way of politics. The resident manager of the housing complex had always wanted to be involved with the agency. However, due to the confidential nature of counseling, I felt it best to restrict her involvement outside of the office. After she became insistent that she be provided with a key to our office and have access to our files and I was unable to receive the needed support from the housing authority, I closed the Hollywood Courts site and extended our Old National office. We invited all our clients from that office to join us on Old National.

Before we closed that office, the agency had empowered the clients in that area having offered individual counseling, family counseling, tutoring, parenting groups, a G.E.D. Program, the P.E.A.C.H. Program, psychological evaluations and school advocacy. Hand-in-Hand Counseling Services, Inc. had enhanced the lives of more than three hundred individuals in the eighteen months that we were housed in that community.

After approximately six months of being involved with Hand-in-Hand Counseling Services, Inc., Dr. White's office received wide recognition on its work with children who were experiencing difficulties with attention deficit disorders. It placed additional restraints on her time and she was unable to continue her supervision of the Hand-in-Hand staff. She had often stated that were it not for Hand-in-Hand Counseling Services, Inc., our target population would not be served. Traditionally our population (Medicaid recipients) would not go to an office for therapy. The level of professionalism, commitment and care as displayed by our staff was desperately needed. While she was no longer available to us, she recommended a Dr. Shirley Perkins.

Our staff put forth an extensive effort to locate a Medicaid doctor. We interviewed a number of their providers who had responded to our advertisements. We wanted to make sure that our clients would get the quality of services they deserved.

During the period of time between providers, the agency continued to see clients with no reimbursement for services. As always, the agency's policy was to not turn anyone away, regardless of his or her ability to pay. Our goals were to unify, to enhance and to empower families. By this time, ninety-five per cent of the referrals to all three of the offices were Medicaid recipients.

Dr. Perkins was very impressed with the services provided by the agency as well as the qualifications of the staff. It was shared with her initially my concerns about the quality of the supervision of the staff at the Brunswick office. She informed me that her responsibilities as a professor at Mansfield College would require a good deal of her time for the first three weeks of her contract. After that, she would fix her schedule so that she would be available to travel to Brunswick every six weeks.

During the course of the interview, it was mentioned that we were anxious to get our doctor in place because we had continued to serve our clients during the period when we had no doctor. Dr. Perkins asked if those same clients were still involved with the agency. When she was informed that they were still active, she stated that they would come under her supervision. Because of her level of confidence with the agency's staff and the procedures put in place by our previous doctor, Dr. Perkins stated that the agency should bill for services rendered because Medicaid allowed for retroactive billing up to three months. She stated that she would review all of the files involved for that period and the agency compensate her for each month, $2,500.00 according to her signed contract, or a total of $7,500.00.

It was very important to me that I obtain a written contract this time because before, there were no written contracts between Hand-in-Hand Counseling Services, Inc. and the Medicaid providers. I decided that any future doctors would have to give me something in writing. While the doctors said the liability was theirs, Medicaid was sending the checks in the name of the agency.

The services provided at the individual locations were meeting specific needs. The feedback received by the agency indicated that families were being reunified and lives were literally being saved. I truly felt the agency was accomplishing those things that God would have it do.

During this period I had finally begun to relax a little. Things were going very well and the agency had reached a point where it was able to hire full time staff. I was in daily contact with the Atlanta office (from school) and the area coordinator, Anne Simpson, was responsible for keeping me abreast of the Brunswick office. The area coordinators (full-time staff) at both offices were expected to maintain daily contact with each other.

Unfortunately, the supervision provided by Dr. Perkins left a lot to be desired. Instead of making the agreed upon trips to Brunswick, she instead developed forms that she could use to keep tract of the clients and supervise the staff and their counseling skills. While this was not my desire, it was more than the agency had received from Dr. Muhammed or Dr. White.

This procedure provided the agency with some kind of documentation to confirm that the staff was following the instructions of the doctor. The procedure gave me a sense of confidence, at last, because I had some kind of documentation to protect the agency from liability. The agency was not making any decisions concerning the procedure with Medicaid, and never had. We were only doing those things as directed by the provider.

Chapter 2

AFTER YOU HAVE DONE ALL YOU CAN,
KEEP TRUSTING

The Investigation

On August 3, 1994, I received a call from the Brunswick office informing me that a Ms. Mabel Green with the Medicaid office had been to visit them asking to see the doctor and review certain files. Carmen Riley, the area coordinator, wanted to know what she should say to them. I informed her that neither the agency nor I had anything to hide . . . Tell her the truth, that the doctor had no set schedule for coming into the office. I informed Carmen to cooperate fully. We gladly provided copies of all the files requested.

After that conversation, I called Dr. Perkins and informed her that Medicaid had contacted the Brunswick office in reference to the doctor. And I suggested that she might want to call Medicaid immediately. She said she was eating dinner and she would call them later on. To my knowledge, she never did.

I had often shared my frustrations (with the staff at each office) about the "laid-back" attitude of the Medicaid doctors. As director of the agency, I paid them, but I was unable to force them to get more involved with our clients. They all talked the talk, but I was raised to believe that actions spoke louder than words. But I continued to tolerate their attitude of indifference because, as our clients constantly reminded us, nobody else seemed to care about them the way the staff at Hand-in-Hand did. And based on my professional dealing with other social service agencies, I was forced to agree with them. So . . . I continued to "put up" with the doctors, and I continued to pray and ask God to give me strength to hold on until another resource could be found to accommodate this population.

A couple of weeks after the Medicaid investigator's visit to the Brunswick office, we were honored with their presence at the Old National office. It was during this conference with Ms. Green that I learned the agency was in violation of the Medicaid policy. Their policy did not permit payment for the kind of services we provided (counseling provided by a behavior specialist and supervised by one of their providers). They only paid for "therapy" conducted by one of their doctors.

Several months passed when one day my husband, Calvin, told me that he had overheard the conversation of some employees of Medicaid while at lunch in the state employees cafeteria. They were saying that I, JoAnn Edwenia Fletcher-Cash and not the agency, was the target of a Medicaid investigation. I was only semi-alarmed because I knew that my brother, James Fletcher, who had at one time been on our staff, was involved in what had been described as an investigation of the largest case of Medicaid fraud in Georgia's history. I felt confident that it must have something to do with that investigation.

My husband and I made contact with my attorney, Jim Gresham, to find out exactly what was going on. Attorney Gresham learned that the Department of Medical Assistance (D.M.A.) had the Federal Bureau of Investigations, (F.B.I) working with them to investigate Medicaid fraud. He scheduled a meeting for all of us to meet at the Old National office.

Attorney Gresham, along with a Mr. Harris and Mr. Smith of the F.B.I. and Ms. Mabel Green with the D.M.A. met with my husband and me. Mr. Harris informed me that we could "by-pass this whole thing" (the investigation), if I would help them get Fletcher (my brother). I told them I would not be able to help them because I did not know anything about what he was doing.

The conference proceeded with them asking questions about the start of the agency and how it became involved with Medicaid. They had subpoenas for several personnel files, client's files; as well as financial records and cancelled checks. We cooperated fully.

After a five-month period of trusting God and holding my breath, I received a call from our attorney. He informed me that he had been in contact with the F.B.I. After carefully checking all the agency's bank records (they subpoenaed all bank statements) the agency had been cleared of any wrongdoing. They stated that we could pick up our records from their office. I asked that they please return our records to us. Mr. Smith "dropped off" our documents one evening on his way home.

Shortly after Dr. Perkins became involved with the agency, she expressed some of her concerns about problems with childcare and personal limitations, which kept her from keeping her commitment to the Brunswick staff. I paid an additional $500.00 a month to her in hopes of helping her work out her obligations so that she could honor her contract with the agency.

After approximately one year, Dr. Perkins terminated her involvement with the agency. Per her contract, she was to make $2,500.00 per month for the supervision of the agency's staff. She was paid $7,500.00 for the three months she allowed the agency to bill retroactively. She was paid an additional $500.00 monthly for ten months in hopes of encouraging her to provide more supervision to the Brunswick office.

Finally I had to accept the fact that, not only was Dr. Perkins not willing to provide "on-site" supervision to the Brunswick staff, she was also negligent with her responsibilities to the staff in Atlanta, as well.

Because I was unable to force her to live up to the contractual agreement, I withdrew the additional $500.00 monthly and wrote her a check for $2500.00. That is when she terminated her contract with the agency.

In an effort to maintain the Brunswick office, I continued with my attempts to locate a provider who "seemed to have time" for our clients. I knew that a local person would have the best opportunity to provide the quality of service that our clientele deserved and I desired. I was extremely pleased when a local resident of Brunswick and a supporter of the agency, Riley Hawkins, informed me of an African American Medicaid provider who was returning to live in the area, Dr. Ted Manning.

Anne Simpson, the Atlanta area coordinator, and I both interviewed Dr. Manning . . . stating our expectations and sharing our frustrations concerning the previous providers. While stressing the importance of the agency being in compliance with Medicaid rules and regulations, Dr. Manning stated "young ladies, I have been a provider for Medicaid for more than thirty years . . . I know what I am doing."

The future for the Brunswick office suddenly seemed bright. Dr. Manning agreed to work along with Dr. Hamilton and the counselors, who would concentrate on the non-Medicaid clients. African-Americans would not only provide services but males as well. This seemed to be a win-win situation.

Dr. Paul Utterly, who had been on the Medicaid Board responsible for writing their policies and procedures, was hired to work part-time along with Dr. Mary Johnson at the Old National Office. Each was available on a part-time basis. And having both providers allowed the agency to continue to provide their full-time services now that we understood that the sessions had to be conducted by the doctors. Once I learned that counselors could not provide individual and family sessions and be paid by Medicaid, they were assigned to certain groups to assist the provider with behavior management.

A few months after Dr. Manning joined the Brunswick staff, they continued to make plans for a 'family unification picnic' that was to be held at a local park. This was an effort to use the holistic approach and involve parents, along with their children. Group sessions would include the topics: improving positive self-esteem, anger management, alternatives to domestic violence, and sibling rivalry. These topics were to be led by Dr. Manning with the assistance of Dr. Hamilton and other counselors. Because the provider conducted these groups, they were to be billed to Medicaid.

Approximately seventy-five local families as well as approximately thirty staff and adolescents (mentors) from the Atlanta office attended the picnic. Group sessions were held for the clients and the staff was available to answer questions from the parents. The mayor of Brunswick also had his representative in attendance to present a "Proclamation" to the agency.

About two weeks after the picnic, I held a meeting with the Brunswick staff, to address their concerns about the agency's involvement with Medicaid. Dr. Hamilton suggested that the agency place a 'moratorium' on billing until we could get someone from Medicaid to meet face-to-face with the staff. The staff stated that they would continue providing services to our clients until this meeting took place.

Dr. Manning expressed his displeasure with the idea of a 'moratorium.' He stated that with the procedures he had put in place in the offices as well as the training he was planning to provide for the staff . . . there was no reason for concern.

I again shared my frustrations with the staff in Brunswick about not having access to a Medicaid representative. Whenever I telephoned that agency and asked to speak with one of its representatives, I was asked for my provider number. When I informed them that I was not a provider, they stated that in order for me to ask questions about Medicaid's policies and procedures, I must be one of their providers. Therefore, I was never able to receive any direct communication from the Department of Medical Assistance. I only had the directions from their providers that had been hired by the agency.

I agreed to place a moratorium on billing for any more services until I could meet face-to-face with a Medicaid representative. I also thanked the staff for their support as well as their continued commitment to our clients.

The week following this meeting, I wrote a letter to Attorney Gresham informing him of this moratorium and asked him to assist me in setting up this face-to-face meeting with Medicaid. While sitting at the desk in the reception area in the Old National office, I was in the process of asking God to fix things for us because I did not want the Brunswick staff lingering . . . providing services and I not be able to compensate them because of the moratorium. Suddenly I heard the fax machine.

When I walked into our business office to check the fax, I had received faxed resignations from each of the Brunswick staff, with the exception of Dr. Manning. In a way, this was an answer to my prayer because I no longer had to be concerned about that staff lingering and my inability to pay them.

The Brunswick office remained closed for several months until Dr. Fred Brown (who had been recommended by Dr. Utterly) was hired, along with a new coordinator. I interviewed Dr. Brown, a local provider who had a private practice on St. Simons Island. I informed him that the agency was a target of a Medicaid investigation. I updated him on our situation and held nothing back from him.

I informed Dr. Brown that previously, I had "trusted the doctor" to give me directions concerning Medicaid's rules and regulation. But now that I know the rules, the provider would have to be the one to provide the services. I was still willing to provide a counselor to sit in the group for behavior management.

I felt the strong need to have an African American counselor to be involved in the groups after I saw the disciplinary problems, which resulted from Dr. Utterly's inability to maintain behavior control. He had been working with a group of three to five year olds at the Old National office, and somehow, they managed to lock him out of the counseling room during his group. And you should just see him trying to work with African American adolescents. It was a real joke!

During this time, the agency had also hired another provider, Dr. Mary Johnson, to work part-time alone with Dr. Utterly. After several months, Dr. Johnson terminated her services with the agency. Her primary reasons for leaving were that she wanted a guaranteed salary and more hours than the agency could afford at that time. This was not considered because the number of clients participating in her groups had decreased tremendously. I interpreted that to mean that, with her, their needs were not being met.

That summer, Dr. Marlene Speed, a close friend, talked me into offering a summer enrichment program for children age three to twelve years old. She knew that my area of expertise was working with adolescents, however, because this was her specialty, she reminded me of the need for intervention with this younger population. And she had written an eight weeks curriculum, designed to encourage, enhance and empower these youngsters.

Her topics dealt with building self-esteem, anger management and cooperative play, sibling rivalry, positive interactions and effective parenting for their parents and guardians. We rented a corridor in a church in Riverdale, Georgia, with a playground, to house this program. Head Start teachers were hired to participate in the groups to assist with behavior management and Dr. Utterly was the therapist or provider.

The facility was gorgeous, the staff was competent and forty children were accepted in the program. However, I cried a lot during the eight weeks period because I saw just how much good could come from a program such as this one. But when you had a provider who seemed to have absolutely no genuine interest in the children and not even be able to tolerate the little children's touch, I asked God just how long was He going to let me have to tolerate this kind of doctor. Surely Medicaid had a provider who was nurturing and caring. And I was not going to stop until I found one, otherwise this population, without some intervention, would continue to deteriorate.

God answered my prayers by sending Dr. Christopher San Miguel. He was recommended by Dr. Utterly and began working with the agency on a part-time basis with him to service the needs of our Medicaid clientele.

Because Medicaid only paid for services that were provided by one of their providers, it was financially advantageous for the agency to offer services in the form of groups. The agency rented a house on Memorial Drive in S.E. Atlanta to accommodate the adolescents participating in our groups. And Dr. San Miguel and Dr. Utterly were our providers, along with staff that participated in the group for behavior management and control.

The program made a tremendous impact on the lives of the individuals involved. And due to non-emergency transportation, the impact was far reaching. Children were attending the program from as far as fifty miles away.

Meanwhile things were off to a very slow start in Brunswick with Dr. Brown. He enjoyed providing the services for the groups and had his secretary from his St. Simons Island office type his group notes. And he worked diligently with the office staff to encourage the clients to return to the office and continue their services.

This is when I learned that the clients were not returning to Hand-in-Hand because Dr. Manning had opened his own private office and had hired some of the agency's former staff. They were recruiting the children to his new office, a violation of one of the clauses in his contract with Hand-in-Hand Counseling Services, Inc.

I finally had a committed provider to work in the Brunswick office . . . but no clientele. I was forced to close the Brunswick office after approximately six years and serving about four hundred clients.

At the end of our eight weeks program on Memorial Drive, I made a decision that was extremely difficult. I fired Dr. Utterly. He was only willing to remain in the group as long as a counselor, who was supposed to be present only for behavior management, was interacting with the clients. THAT WAS NOT WHAT MEDICAID SAID WAS TO BE DONE! If the counselor "slipped out" of the group for any reason, Dr. Utterly left it as well. He had no problem leaving the clients unsupervised.

Also, I had real concerns with his "record keeping" techniques. He would scribble client's progress on little pieces of paper but failed to document the client's files. And then he refused to leave the client's files in the office but insisted instead on keeping them in the trunk of his car. And he was a member of the board who helped write Medicaid guidelines.

Dr. San Miguel worked to help keep the agency afloat. He had a genuine love and sensitivity for our clients like none of the other providers. One day I was assisting in the group for behavior control. He was leading a group, which consisted of ten to twelve year olds. One of the boys started to talk about how much he missed his mother because she was "away". After Dr. San Miguel questioned him about his feelings, it was revealed that the boy's mother was in prison.

Suddenly several of the other children opened up and began to talk about their mothers also being away. Of the ten clients participating in the group seven of their mothers were "away". The boy who initiated the conversation started to cry, saying he missed his mom and wanted her back home.

At once it seemed that all of the others started to cry, too. Dr. San Miguel left his chair and kneeled down and hugged the little boy who first started crying. Then all of the others joined in and piled on Dr. San Miguel, who by this time was sitting on the floor, cuddling and rocking the pile of boys! I could not hold back my tears, and left the group. None of the children left the room behind me. I thanked God that finally we had a Medicaid provider who cared!

Without warning, the D.M.A. withheld the checks for services payable to Hand-in-hand Counseling Services, Inc. We learned that, even though our current provider (Dr. San Miguel) had no involvement with the irregularities in procedure, which led to the fraud charges, the D.M.A. refused to issue further checks to the agency with those charges pending.

I had come to the end of my road. The agency no longer had the different financial resources as when we first started. While we continued to have the support and numerous referrals from the juvenile courts and the Department of Family and Children Services, they no longer contracted to pay for their referrals. They too, encouraged their referrals to use their Medicaid benefits.

Knowing that God can do anything, and that He was still in charge of this situation, I refused to quit. Instead I moved the office to another site (management sold the building we were in) and had new brochures, business cards and letterhead printed. It had been revealed to me the new direction the agency needed to pursue.

But first, I had to go to Brunswick and take care of a little misunderstanding regarding the fraud investigation. Something was wrong with this system. Somebody needed to hear from me, allow me to show him or her my documentation explaining why I did what I did! I felt confident that this error would be corrected.

There was no elaborate scheme to commit fraud that would be so wide spread that it covered the entire state. My explanation was simple; God had smiled on Hand-in-Hand Counseling Services, Inc. and I was very honored and humbled by it!

The Indictment

One day in March 1997, I received a call from Attorney Jim Gresham informing me that the D.M.A. wanted to meet with me and ask me some questions. I was excited because, finally I was being given an opportunity to tell my side of the story. We were scheduled to meet at the D.M.A.'s office in Tucker, Georgia. My husband and I met Attorney Gresham in the parking lot of the juvenile court and he drove us to the meeting.

Once we arrived at the office, Attorney Gresham stated that he and I would probably be the only ones allowed in the meeting. After about a ten-minute wait, we were led back to the conference room occupied by four men and two women. Among those present was Mabel Green, the investigator who had visited the Brunswick office as well as attended the conference when the Federal Bureau of Investigation interviewed me.

Attorney Gresham was called out of the conference room the minute we entered and I remained 'standing' in the room with Ms. Green and the others who were gathering their things to leave. Attorney Gresham returned minutes later and said, "let's get out of here. Those S.O.B.'s have already decided to indict you on two counts of Medicaid Fraud. I was stunned because, so far, I still had not been given an opportunity to explain or express my side of the story or even answer any of their questions.

The indictment had come, not from Fulton or Dekalb counties, but Brunswick and Glynn County because of the billing under Dr. Perkins and Dr. Manning's supervision. Attorney Gresham felt fairly confident that the charges would not have any merit because a person is supposed to be indicted in the county where their crime occurred. Since the indictment stated the crime as "the billing of Medicaid" . . . the fraud, none of the billing occurred in Glynn County. It was believed that Glynn County had no jurisdiction to pursue these charges.

Attorney Gresham told me I had two days from the date of indictment to turn myself in to the Glynn County Detention Center or a warrant would be issued for my arrest. Attorney Gresham also told me that I would be held pending a $10,000.00 cash bond and $25,000.00 property bond. He informed me that it would be too expensive to hire him to represent me because of the distance. Brunswick is located 300 miles from Atlanta. He suggested that I hire a good local attorney.

When I started to look for an attorney in the Brunswick area, I spoke with several local individuals asking for their recommendations. None of them recommended the attorney that I chose, Attorney Keith Williams.

I had met Mr. Williams several years ago. My aunt, Viola Hazzard, was desperately trying to find out some information concerning her daughter, Joelynn Allen's drug conviction and sentencing. Her efforts had led her into a brick wall.

One week while in Brunswick, my aunt shared her frustrations with me. She did not know anything about the procedure for securing her desired information, but she did have a name of someone who was in a position to help . . . Keith Williams, Glynn County Public Defender. I called Mr. Williams and learned that he was in private practice and scheduled an appointment for us to meet.

I was very impressed with Mr. Williams' level of professionalism and caring he displayed with my aunt. While sitting in his office and listening to him minister to my aunt, I thought, if I ever need a lawyer, "you are the one."

I prayed and asked God to show me if Mr. Williams was not the right lawyer for me. When I called, I informed him that I had called for recommendations from some locals and none of them called his name. I also told him I asked God to show me if he was not the right lawyer for me. The locals felt that he was not experienced enough to handle the case, but since God had not told me that, I was trusting God because He had not failed me yet.

It is important to mention that, while my involvement with Hand-in-Hand had been on a part-time basis, my work with the school system was still in tact. I was still carrying out my duties to the best of my ability. While I had made my supervisors aware of a limited amount of what was happening to me, I never imagined it going this far to my being indicted. Many of my associates from the school system were employed by the agency.

As I prepared to go to Brunswick to meet with Mr. Williams, I had a heart-to-heart talk with God. I reminded Him that, a long time ago, I had made Him the head of my life and I was totally depending on Him to work this out. Because I knew that nothing was too hard for Him. I did not even go by the bank. I had about $69.00 in my purse when I left Atlanta headed to Brunswick. I was in the same position David was in when he went out to meet Goliath . . . all I had was "a rag and a rock." But with God, that was enough.

During my meeting with Mr. Williams, I assured him that, for me, this entire situation was only a test of my faith. . . just like Job, God's friend.

After bringing him up to date on the agency's involvement with Medicaid and the measures put forth to assure compliance, I was confident that I had nothing to fear with this indictment. Once the truth was known, this would all be over. Then I asked him to represent me in court the following day. Mr. Williams first told me that there were no guarantees as to the outcome, but he felt that I had an excellent chance to be cleared of the charges. He then informed me that his fee would be $7,500.00 and he would need one half of the fee before he could represent me the following day.

After the shock of the situation began to wear off, I asked God just how He was going to handle this? Then I was led to contact Rev. E.C. Tillman for assistance. Once I updated him on the situation, he stated that he would talk to the judge, due to his having personal knowledge of my character and my family's involvement in his church . . . he married me and buried my mother. He would try and get my bond more reasonable.

I was staying with my friend Gloria and we had prayer over the situation. Overnight, it was necessary for me to come up with $3750.00 and all I had was about $69.00. This situation reminded me of the Bible story talking about God feeding the multitude with two fish and five loaves of bread. I needed Him to work another miracle.

While considering my options, Gloria suggested that I ask her grandmother, Linda James, for a loan. I was a bit hesitant to do so because I knew that, for years, I was not one of her grandmother's favorite people. She did not care for me and let me know it every chance she got.

You see, for years, prior to Hand-in-Hand, when I went to Brunswick on visits, I would always go to Gloria's house and get her to hang out with me. This did not sit well with her grandmother because Gloria has, for quite some time, been battling cancer. And her grandmother was overly protective of her. She did not want Gloria going to clubs and hanging out at all hours. And Gloria would "hang-out" with me every time I came home.

When we arrived at Ms. James' house, she was baby sitting for a two year old. Gloria told her that we needed to talk to her. I told her my situation and that I needed to come up with $3750.00 by tomorrow. She asked me how much I was asking her to loan me. I told her that I would appreciate anything that she could do. She said, "Gloria, get my shoes, we got to go to the bank." She loaned me $2000.00. I thanked her and I thanked God.

About two hours later, I went to my sister-in-law, Marion Moses' house. I discussed the situation with her because I was considering calling Cecelia

"Renelda" Bennett, another sister-in-law. Marion suggested that because Renelda had been ill, I should call Gloria Cash, my sister-in-law in Maryland.

After calling Gloria in Landover, Maryland and telling her about the situation, she said, "I am cooking right now, give me about forty minutes." She said, "you might need something extra so I am wiring you $2000.00." I thanked her, and I thanked God. I now had $250.00 more than I needed three hours after I learned that I needed it. God simply showed His awesome ability to make a way out of no way! With Him, a rag and a rock are sufficient.

I was scheduled "to turn myself in" the following morning before eleven o'clock. Mr. Williams had asked me to meet him at his office prior to my going to the Glynn County Detention Center. The center was in walking distance of his office . . . the next block over, to be exact. I paid him one half of his fee, $3,750.00 as requested.

While meeting with Mr. Williams, Gwen, an acquaintance from high school, came bursting in the office, after learning from my sister-in-law that I was there. She worked as a jailer at the detention center and overheard an officer preparing to type a bench warrant for my arrest.

Gwen grabbed me by my hand and we just started running to the center. When we got to the door, she pushed me inside. Another female officer walked pass me and said, "don't be afraid, I have been asked to look out for you."

After I had been read my rights, fingerprinted and mug shot taken, I was booked into the detention center around twelve o'clock. The duty officer told me to stay seated until he had a chance to eat his lunch and he would finish my processing. He assured me that I would not have to sit there long because he could only allow me to remain there for a certain time period.

As I sat in the booking area, waiting for the officer to put me in a cell, I started asking God why was He letting this go this far? Surely I would not have to go to jail for doing everything in my power to make sure that we did everything right! I reminded myself that this must just be a test of my faith. And I made up my mind, right then and there, whatever the test, I am going to pass it, because I am going to continue to trust God.

While sitting in the booking area, I started to notice that different officers seemed to be coming by to have a look at me. I later learned that to have a $10,000.00 cash bond and $25,000.00 property bond meant that you were really "big time" and of interest. Finally the duty officer asked me, "Ms. Cash, what did you do? I told him my situation, I trusted the doctors but I had been charged because I owned the business.

I continued to pray, telling God that I was scared, but I was going to continue to trust Him. Just to be sure that He was still with me, I asked Him to show me a sign by not allowing "them" to put me in a cell.

The 'duty officer' finished his lunch and started to look at his watch. He then finished processing me into the facility. Each time he got up to start towards me to take me to a cell, something happened to delay him such as new bookings, an argument in the hallway, something.

As I sat there in the lobby of the booking area in the detention center, I started laughing, thanking God for His goodness and mercy. You see, every time the duty officer started in my direction, something would interfere with his getting to me. He even stated, more than once, "I can't believe this." As a result of the many distractions, I sat in that chair for about six hours and was never put into a holding cell.

Shortly before six 6 o'clock that evening, I was told that I had a visitor and was taken to one of the visitation booths. Rev. Tillman came to visit me and informed me that he had spoken to the judge handling my case. Since he vouched for my character, the judge waived the $10,000.00 cash bond. And I now only needed a $25,000.00 property bond to be released.

About half an hour after Rev. Tillman left, Mr. Williams came to visit. He stated that he had an appointment to talk to the judge about my bond. He also informed me that my husband was putting up our house for the property bond. However, my release would be delayed because our property was located outside of Glynn County and I would probably have to stay in jail for at least twenty-four hours until all of the information had been verified.

After Mr. Williams left me, I remained in that visitation booth for what seemed like forever... almost two hours. At first, while sitting there, I started to cry. And then the song, "Lord I'll Go" entered my heart and I started to sing it. I was really having church, and knew that God had not left me. Suddenly a female officer looked in to where I was and asked, "what are you doing in here." I told her that I had been brought here for visitation. The officer apologized for my being left alone for so long, but stated that the shift had changed. Since my processing had not been completed, the staff was unaware that I was even in their facility. I was taken back to my chair.

After sitting for another fifteen minutes, I asked permission to make my one phone call and dialed Gloria's number. I updated her on the situation and told her that I might be held in jail for twenty-four hours because our property was located out of town.

An hour later, the officers told me that my bond had been posted and that I was free to leave. Gloria had shown up at the detention center about twenty minutes after I contacted her, with the deeds to her house (a local address) in her purse. She put up her house for me! Praise God . . . that thirty year-old prophecy had come to pass.

When I got to the parking lot, my husband Calvin, my sister-in-law Marion, and Gloria were waiting for me. Gloria gave me an aspirin and a Pepsi and they whisked me away . . . just like television.

The following day, Calvin and I returned to Atlanta. On our way back, we stopped in Statesboro, Georgia, at Georgia Southern University, where our son was attending college. To this day, that is one of the most difficult tasks I have had in my life . . . to have to tell my son that I had been in jail. The Cash family cried together.

My next unpleasant task was to return to work and notify my employer (of more than twenty years) of my indictment and possible pending trial. The support given, especially from my immediate supervisor, Linda Dickson, was tremendous. After sharing with her some of the documentation received from the doctors giving the agency directions, Ms. Dickson also felt that this was all a terrible mistake and would be cleared up shortly.

Several months later, it was necessary for me to return to Brunswick for a Probable Cause Hearing. Gloria picked me up from the airport in Jacksonville, Florida for the short trip on to Brunswick. This is when I learned the full impact of the situation. With my continuous employment with the school system and my regarding the agency as my mission and not a source of income, I failed to realize the full extent of the agency's growth.

It was at this hearing that I learned the agency had served families in twenty-seven cities due to the use of non-emergency transportation. And because of this widespread involvement, the prosecutor had concluded that I, JoAnn Edwenia Fletcher-Cash, had set up this elaborate scheme designed to cover the entire state of Georgia and defraud the Medicaid system.

While I was shocked at the implications, I could not help but thank God for all His marvelous works. He had truly answered my prayers by using the agency to meet the needs of those people who were sick and tired of being sick and tired.

Gloria and a friend of hers, Pam, took me back to Jacksonville, Florida to catch my plane back to Atlanta. We were having church, praising God while listening to a tape by Bishop T.D. Jakes, as we rode along. But before

46

I caught the flight, they wanted me to meet a lady who was a prayer warrior, someone who could get a prayer through to God . . . and to eat some barbecue from this special rib place.

When we first arrived at the lady's house, she was not at home. After sitting out in front of her house, waiting about thirty minutes, we decided to go to the rib place, eat, and come back. And that is what we did.

Once we returned to the lady's house, she still was not home. We decided to wait on her and she arrived about five minutes later. Gloria had been inspired by this lady before and knew, just what she could do. I had approximately two and one half hours before I needed to get to the airport.

After I updated her on my situation, she first gave me several scriptures to read and told me the best time of day for me to read them. And then she began to pray and we had a visitation with the Holy Spirit. Once things calmed down a little bit, I looked at my watch and was startled to see that it was 3:20 p.m. My flight back to Atlanta was scheduled to leave at 3:40 p.m. I had twenty minutes before my flight was scheduled for "take-off."

I told Gloria that I needed to use the telephone to call Margaret Martin "Lynn," my sister-in-law. She was set to pick me up from the Atlanta airport but I was not going to be able to catch that plane. Gloria and the lady both assured me that the plane would not leave without me.

As we were leaving the lady's house, it started to rain. She told us that the airport was about ten minutes away. It rained very hard and traffic was slowed. We arrived at the airport and as I was getting out of the van, my watch indicated it was 3:40 p.m. on the dot. I grabbed my larger piece of luggage and Gloria got the smaller one. As we entered the airport, I noticed that the sun had started to shine.

When I walked up to the Delta Airlines counter and presented my ticket to the agent, he stated that he was sorry. I was too late. My plane was scheduled to "taxi" five minutes ago. I asked what gate did it load from, and he said it loaded from gate twenty-four. From where I was standing, I could see gate three. I had missed the plane. Gloria, standing behind me said, "you have not missed that plane." She took the larger piece of luggage and told me to take the smaller piece and run on to the gate. She said she would be right behind me.

Have you ever seen the commercial with O.J. Simpson running through the airport? That is exactly how I felt! And the strange thing about it was . . . the airport was almost deserted, on a nice Saturday afternoon in August.

As I ran up to the ticket agent at gate twenty-four and asked for my flight, the agent was in the process of telling me that I was too late when the stewardess at the boarding gate said, Mrs. Cash, we are waiting for you!" I boarded the plane, wet with sweat and exhausted.

I dreaded trying to put my luggage in the overhead storage because my arms felt like lead and I was sure that I would not be able to lift them. As I approached my seat, the young man who was sitting in the seat next to mine, stood up and took one piece of the luggage out of my hand at the same time the stewardess walked up behind me and took the other piece of luggage. They placed them in the overhead storage for me. I did not even have to raise my arms.

Once I sat down, the young man offered me his handkerchief to wipe my face. He then asked, "who are you?" I just looked at him, prepared to introduce myself. He said I am a "frequent-flyer" and right now I am on my way to meet my wife in Rome, Italy. I have never sat on a 747 jet and waited for it to "taxi" as long as I have today. He further stated, "If I didn't know any better, I would think that it waited for you. I answered and said, "it did" God held it up for me! Right then and there, I thanked Him!

Mr. Williams filed a motion for a Change of Venue Hearing. It was his contention that if the state was going to pursue these charges (Medicaid Fraud, two counts) against me, then my indictment should take place in the county where the crime occurred. That would have been Fulton County, because all of our billing was done from our Old National Office.

My family and I suffered a great deal of anxiety waiting for closure to this matter because the scheduled hearing was postponed several times due to the illness of the presiding judge. Finally the hearing was scheduled for February 2, 1998 and due to the continued illness of the presiding judge, my case was assigned to Judge Wilma Anderson.

I made my supervisors at work aware that I had to attend this hearing in Brunswick and informed them that I would be absent for about one week. I straightened my office desk as I usually would on any Friday. By the time I left the school building, all of the other staff had already left. The custodian was still there, but I did not see him.

Camellia Moore, a long-time friend, had been giving me support throughout this situation. She was the director of Alternate Life Paths Program, Inc. (A.L.P.P.), a program designed to work with troubled adolescents and young adults. She was also a new attorney. I had been her supervisor twenty years ago when she moved to Metropolitan Atlanta from New York to work with the school system. She was employed as a Behavior Disorder (B.D.) teacher in one of the classes under my supervision. As a matter of fact, during that period, James Pencock, Ms. Beddington's grandson, was in her class.

She and I had maintained an intermittent relationship since her move south. Our relationship was renewed, with contacts on an almost daily basis because of these pending charges against me. Also I needed to borrow some female adolescents from her program.

I had written an abstinence-based teenage pregnancy prevention curriculum outline and asked a close friend, Phyl Macon, to take my outline and develop it into an effective preventive tool for adolescents. Camellia agreed to allow some female adolescents from her program to help us "get the bugs" out of the curriculum. Another friend, Judy Raines, provided some valuable assistance.

One day, while I was visiting Camellia's program, she introduced me (Director, Hand-in-Hand Counseling Services, Inc.) to several of her staff members. She paid me probably the biggest compliment of my life . . . " I would like for you to meet the lady who introduced me to Jesus!

Camellia took an interest in my case and I shared with her all of the documentation I had received from the Medicaid providers. She contacted Mr. Williams, my attorney in Brunswick, and volunteered her services to assist him in my defense.

When it was time for me to attend the "Change of Venue" Hearing, my neighbor, Teresa Booker gave me a roundtrip Buddy Pass from Delta Airlines to fly into Savannah, Georgia. Camellia flew to Savannah with me, and from there she rented a car and we drove to Brunswick. The two of us stayed at Gloria's house, although she had planned to get her a hotel room.

After arriving at the courthouse first thing that Monday morning, (February 2, 1998), we had to wait until mid-day before we learned the outcome of the judge's ruling. Due to continued illness of the presiding Superior Court Judge, my case had been assigned to a Circuit Judge . . . Wilma Anderson. She ruled that Glynn County was indeed the proper county to handle this indictment because "the targeted Medicaid clients as well as the office were located in that district." Our next procedure was to participate in the selection of my jury. I was actually going on trial for two counts of Medicaid fraud.

Terence Hatcher, my administrative assistant, at Hand-in-Hand Counseling Services, Inc. had done a tremendous job helping me gather and organize a three ring binder with all of the documentation necessary to prove that my actions, as the agency's director, were based on the instructions given to me from the Medicaid provider. He too, was confident that this misunderstanding would soon be corrected, especially with his first hand knowledge of the documentation that would prove the reasons for my actions.

This had not yet turned into a nightmare for me. I started to think, O.K. Lord, I know that You are in charge of this entire situation. I just bet You are going to use me to expose just how little the typical Medicaid provider really cares about its clientele. I am going to be used to help revamp the entire Medicaid system! O.K., I'm with You, so go ahead and use me any way You want! I have put all my trust in You.

The Trial and Conviction

Once it had been established that Glynn County was the correct district to pursue my indictment for Medicaid Fraud and the "Change of Venue" motion had been denied, the next procedure was the selection of a jury. The Constitution of the United States entitled me, as an American citizen, to be tried by a jury of my peers.

This jury pool consisted of approximately fifty individuals. . . Caucasians, Asians, and four African Americans, two males and two females. I was not overly concerned about the members of the jury because, for me, it was very clear that there had been major misunderstanding. I was feeling confident that, if twelve individuals, regardless of color, with an I.Q. of at least twelve could hear my side of the story, then it would be known that I was innocent. I did not set out to defraud anyone, as the prosecution had contended.

My anxiety was based on whether or not the Medicaid providers would be honest in their testimony . . .that I was following their directions. If the providers stated that I worked independent of their instructions or without their knowledge, then I would be in a position where it would be my word against theirs. They could easily be less than truthful and say that they were unaware of what I was doing and had no part in it . . . that the agency's use of their provider number, used for billing the D.M.A., was unauthorized by them. That was my biggest fear. But I was trusting God that would not happen.

Mr. Williams and Camellia explained the process of jury selection. It was not totally foreign because in the past, I had sat on several juries. And they encouraged my participation in the process. But I was confident in their ability and pretty much left the jury selection to them.

Just before the actual selection process began, the judge called for a fifteen minutes recess. I was glad because Gloria was not able to come to court that morning and I had promised that I would keep her informed of the happenings. But first, I decided that I had better go on to the restroom. After leaving the restroom, I called Gloria and gave her an update . . . I was going to trial!

When I returned to the courtroom, I asked Camellia if I could borrow a dime from her to repay the one I had just borrowed from the lady in the hall. Camellia asked me whom I had borrowed it from. When I pointed to the lady who had loaned me the dime, Camellia frowned and said, "JoAnn, you were not supposed to talk with her." It could be seen as possible jury tampering.

She then informed Mr. Williams who agreed with her perception of the situation.

Mr. Williams took the dime from me and repaid the lady. I then confessed to him and Camellia that the other African American female potential juror was in the restroom with me. We struck up a conversation and she told me that she had a terrible toothache. I gave her two Tylenol from my purse and she thanked me for them.

When Mr. Williams informed the judge of my actions, the lady with the toothache and the one who loaned me the dime were stricken from the pool and eliminated as possible jurors. I had really shot myself in the foot due to my ignorance!

Once the tedious task of jury selection had been completed, a jury of twelve local men and women would determine my fate. Only one African American male was on the jury and the other one would be serving as an alternate.

Prior to going to trial, the prosecutor had offered me "a deal" -- six months prison sentence and five years probation, if I were to enter a guilty plea. By doing so, I would be admitting that I went along with something that I knew was wrong. But I never once considered doing so. There had been no scheme, but a misinterpretation of the rules. And I was more than willing to pay my portion of the reimbursement, along with the providers.

Immediately I was shocked to see that the D.M.A. did not send representatives of their different departments (like the Accounting Department and the Policies and Procedures Department) to testify against me . . . but the Directors themselves. I could not help but to think that the town's close proximity to "The Golden Isles," Jekyll Island, St. Simons island and Sea island, had more to do with their presence than I did. And they had also brought from Atlanta, three of my most trusted staff to testify against me.

The D.M.A. confirmed my feelings of their overall incompetence. For example, the individual who testified as the director of the Policies and Procedures Department was not able to even appear to have an accurate knowledge of the most recent changes and updates with their rules and regulations. Her testimony showed her as being less than competent and I remember listening and thinking "oh no, she could not work at Hand-in-Hand, because we all were "a cut above the rest."

My opinion did not change after hearing the testimony of the remainder of the state's employees. They displayed large, colorful, and attractive charts to paint an ugly picture to illustrate how the state's money had been wasted. Facts were distorted. And some of the expenses, they just did not like.

For a period of eleven months when my mother was ill, bedridden, and living with me, I paid her sitter from the agency's account. I felt justified in doing so because, first, God had given "me" the business and she was MY mother. And second, mother had been an initial investor in the agency. I felt very thankful to be able to pay the sitter and I still was not paying myself a salary.

Many times my husband would complain that, for me, Hand-in-Hand was a "hobby" and not a business because I would not pay myself a salary. He would say that I was crazy because I paid out the majority of the income either to the staff in salaries and bonuses or doing something to enhance and empower the agency. Cash said, "common sense ought to tell you to put some of the income in your own house." He also said that the agency was MY mission and not his, . . .if you can't pay yourself, pay me!"

I had drafted him several months earlier to be the facilitator and lead the agency's weekly Domestic Violence Group. I knew he would do a fantastic job with it, especially since it would give him an opportunity to use his law degree. After approximately six months of weekly volunteer services, the agency began to compensate him for his services rendered.

One of my sister-in-laws, Margaret "Lynn" Martin, had worked in accounting at Spelman College before having to go on disability. She would help out at the office; either by substituting for our receptionist and/or assisting me with balancing the agency's checkbook, and she also helped me with the accuracy of the payroll before it was sent to our accountant. Her services were compensated as well.

When something "real special" had occurred and I was especially proud of the agency's accomplishments, I would compensate myself by purchasing a gold bracelet (between $100.00 and $300.00) or an outfit from my favorite boutique. And this occurred only occasionally. These items were purchased from the agency's account as well, instead of paying myself a salary. In the ten-year history of the agency, this was done no more than twenty times. And I, as the owner of the agency, was the only one authorized to write checks on the agency bank account.

Overall, when summarizing my trial, which lasted four days, there were three things that really stand out in my mind. I also recall the manner in which my attorney dealt with me. He had a personal crisis occur and was forced to meet me at Gloria's house late at night to try to prepare me for the next part of the trial. At times, I felt like he was doing me a favor instead of his being my paid attorney because his total fee of $7,500.00 had been paid in full at tremendous sacrifice to my family.

First, as previously stated, the level of competence of the state employees was embarrassing to me as an employer. Having been required, on many occasions, to take the stand and give sworn testimony in my capacity with the school system and previous employment as a probation officer with the juvenile court, I knew the expectations of courts, in general. Not one of the state's four or five witnesses presented themselves very well.

The second thing that comes to mind about the trail is the viciousness, distortions, and out right lies presented by two of the agency's most valued former employees. My mother had often warned me about my lack of perception when it came to other people. She often said, "JoAnn, you take people to heart . . . you need to learn how to feed people out of a long handle spoon, then it will be more difficult for them to hurt you. The two employees who had been my staunchest supporters, Lennie Wilson and Anne Simpson were now my biggest critics.

Last but not least, the third occurrence was the most surprising of them all. And that was the testimony of the previous Medicaid providers. Only three of the four providers involved with the agency during the questionable billing period were called to testify. Dr. Muhammad the provider who introduced the agency to Medicaid was not subpoenaed.

Each Provider attempted to explain that their techniques used to supervise the agency's staff were the same techniques taught to them as part of their graduate training to become doctors. And they stated that the American Psychological Association sanctioned their training. The providers stated that they were confident that their supervision techniques were in accordance with Medicaid's Policies and Procedures.

Only one of the three providers testified that he did not have full knowledge of how the agency was billing Medicaid with his provider number. This was the same provider, who during the initial interview for the position assured Anne and me that he knew all of Medicaid's rules and regulations because he had been a provider for them for more than twenty years. He plead ignorant to the fact that he had granted permission for billing for services on the days that he was not in the office. That was never the agreement, because none of us were aware that Medicaid required the provider to be present at the time services were being rendered. This provider was to supervise the agency's staff, according to his signed contract, by meeting with the counselors and reviewing the client's files.

That provider proved to not have much credibility because Mr. Williams was successful in presenting a client's file to the court bearing the provider's personal signature on a day that the provider had been in the office. He had testified that not only was he not in the office but that he was out of the city. His signature and date proved that his testimony was less than accurate. It was also discovered that, several years ago, that same provider had been convicted, in another state, of Medicaid fraud.

The prosecutor simply lumped all of the monies together that had been paid to the agency to demonstrate the true extent of the deception and tremendous amount received due to my "master-mind scheme" and fraudulent efforts. The majority of the monies discussed had nothing to do with the indictment. And the judge allowed this inclusion to become a part of the trial record.

Several of the counseling staff that had been employed at the Brunswick office was called to testify. Each stated that they had limited knowledge of the business aspects of the agency. But none of them testified to having knowledge of the scheme that I had been accused of. Each expressed some sense of pride in their involvement with Hand-in-Hand Counseling Services, Inc. and the services that had been rendered.

On Thursday night, February 5, 1998, before the last day of the trial, Mr. Williams met with me at Gloria's house in an attempt to prepare me to take the stand. He felt that it was very important that the jury hears from me and I share my side of the story. All during the entire proceeding, he had been concerned because he felt that the prosecutor and the judge had some "personal" dislike for me. They wanted me to show some remorse and admit that I knew, all along, that our techniques for billing Medicaid were not in compliance with their rules and regulations.

I was very disappointed because, during the course of the trial, Mr. Williams failed to enter into evidence any of the numerous memos, notes, and directives that had been made available to him. Terence Hatcher, my administrative assistant, had collected these documents and placed them in a three-ring binder, which verified interactions between the providers and the agency. This information verified the provider's instructions and directives to me, as the agency's director, as well as the counseling staff as it related to Medicaid and the procedures we should follow.

Mr. Williams informed me that he felt it unnecessary to present the documents during his cross-examination because the providers, for the most part, were in agreement with my version of this story. There had been no scheme to defraud, but a misinterpretation of the rules. Therefore, there was no need to challenge their testimony.

Mr. Williams talked about my self-confidence or "an air" that I possessed. He felt that it would be insulting to the court because someone in my position needed to be meek and submissive. They wanted me to crawl before the court! What Mr. Williams failed to realize was that I did not have a meek or submissive bone in my body. My mother had raised me to believe that I was as good as anybody else, not better, but just as good, regardless of color. So, I truly did not know how to act like a "second-class" citizen. And besides, I could not forget all of the good things that the agency had accomplished. Yes, I regretted the misinterpretation of the Medicaid rules, but I was a lot more proud than I was sorry for the services that had been rendered!

While on the stand, I had difficulty attempting to justify to the courts my reason for paying my mother's sitter from the agency's funds. Ms. Laura Wilson, a member of my church, was an experienced sitter and took excellent care of my mother. She deserved nothing less than the best. As the owner of the business, once all the bills and staff had been paid, I felt that I could do whatever I saw fit with the income, especially since I was not paying myself a salary. And to question anything that I had done for my mother was just taking things a bit too far. It was adding insult to injury! And I know that my attitude more than reflected my feelings. I was still grieving the loss of my mother, which had occurred only a year prior to this trial. If money could have saved her, she could have had every dime I owned. And I was not about to feel remorseful about my actions towards her.

Throughout the trial, I failed to focus on what was being said, but instead studied the facial expressions of the jurors, especially the women. Several of them (I felt) realized the position I was in and believed that there had been no deliberate attempt to deceive anyone. It was not as easy for me to get a feeling concerning the male jurors. I did realize that one male, a psychologist, was agitated that he had been selected to be a part of the jury. I felt that he, of all people, could understand just how my situation occurred in the first place.

The jury began its deliberation before lunch. My husband, Camellia and I went to a local restaurant and ate a very enjoyable meal. Little did I know that it would be my 'last supper' as a free citizen for quite some time.

We had been told to be back at the courthouse at 1:00 p.m. Camellia seemed a little restless while Cash seemed irritated. He told me that, "whatever the outcome, things would be different when we get back to Atlanta." I thought he was talking about the amount of time I invested in the agency and others which took away from the family. I listened to what he was saying and did not disagree. I was tired. And having to come to court made me see the need to focus more on "my family."

At approximately 4:00 p.m. we were called back into the courtroom. The jury had reached its decision, guilty on two counts of Medicaid Fraud. I could not believe my ears and I froze in time. Then my spirit left my body!

Mr. Williams asked that the jury be polled individually. As each juror said "GUILTY," I noticed that not one of them looked me in the eyes. As I stood, I could feel myself slowly sinking to the floor. I could hear what was being said, but it was as though I was not part of it, in another world. The last thing I remembered was my husband and Camellia fanning me and removing my jacket.

When I awoke, I was handcuffed to a hospital bed where I had been taken to Glynn Memorial Hospital. There were two deputies outside my door. I was being given medicine intravenously and had ugly bruises on both of my arms. I was being peeped at by several of the staff as well as others who seemed just curious.

Upon my release from the hospital about four hours later, the hospital staff and the deputies attempted to have me sign a statement verifying that I would be responsible for paying the hospital bill. I declined. The two deputies then took me, by police car, to Glynn County Detention Center, where I spent my first night in complete shock!

Wandering in the Wilderness

After being awake all night, I must have dozed off for no more than an hour or so when I heard my name being called. The POD (living quarters) officer was informing me that I needed to get ready for visitation.

As I left my room and entered the "day room" about twelve to fifteen ladies or detainees, crowded around two large tables, stopped their conversations and stared at me. I then noticed that there was a copy of a local newspaper spread out on each table. The article was about my conviction.

I went on to visitation to see my husband and Camellia. He looked like his night had been just as bad as mine. Camellia tried her best to be positive. And to my surprise, one of my teachers from high school, Miss Essie Sheffield, joined us for words of encouragement.

Later that day Mr. Williams came to visit. He seemed as stunned about the conviction as I was. He tried his best to be encouraging but he too looked like he had taken a beating. And he apologized that his efforts had failed. In the meantime he stated that he would pursue getting a bond set so that I could be released to go home with my family until I was sentenced. Then we would immediately file an appeal. Presently the judge had refused to give me a bond. I felt trapped!

When I returned to the POD from my visitation, I asked to read a copy of the newspaper. As I read the words used to describe me as a mastermind, schemer, con artist, manipulator, I felt sure that I was either literally being stabbed in the chest or was having a heart attack. I doubled over the table and was unable to stand. I sobbed.

But God had an angel to watch over me, Linda Kelly. She literally carried me into the laundry room and made a pallet on the floor between the washer and the back door. She joined me on the floor, where she cradled and rocked me and just let me cry for the next three hours. It was then that she presented me with the most powerful weapon to use against fiery darts, a Holy Bible.

The very next day Melody, my "bunkie" (roommate) gave me a copy of From Faith to Faith (a Daily Guide to Victory) by Kenneth and Gloria Copeland. This book, along with my Bible, would prove to be true anchors that would sustain my faith as I began on a journey that would require me to live in a "strange land," in a world outside society. I had a one-way ticket and no way out! Overnight I changed worlds.

For approximately twenty-seven years I had worked (juvenile court and school system) with some of the more difficult children in society. Our paths crossed due to the labels they carried - at-risk, delinquent, disturbed, bad, socially maladjusted, dumb, stupid, but children just the same. Most of their problems were caused by something in their dysfunctional families. And because I was a parent, it was always personally disheartening to see these children merely exist. I could not understand how they got to be the way they were, because surely every parent loved their children. Or so I thought!

Nothing prepared me for this experience and I wandered, simply in awe. God had orchestrated my life so that I would have an opportunity to know, first hand, what kind of events had lead to their deterioration. These were the children who had been written off by society and who could easily be described as "the walking dead." Many of them have a vacant look in their eyes, as though they have simply exited their bodies. They often have no goals, just merely existing. And because they have low or no self-esteem, no ambitions, and no values, they are capable of every harmful act imaginable.

There is no such thing as "authority," no limits whatsoever.

A few years ago experts credited the ills of our youth to the breakdown of the family. This breakdown caused an increase in the number of single mothers and absence of father figures. More often than not, many behaviors could be justified or excused because the father was absent in the life of the child. And it was felt by some that a family headed by a single mother produced "tainted" children.

These children have had to endure hardships because in many instances, they have had to raise themselves. That single mother has had to work extended hours to make ends meet and therefore forced to relinquish many of her parenting duties due to her absence. Some children have had to cook their meals, wash their clothes, and put themselves to bed because their mothers were working late.

We are now faced with a population of children who have no natural parents actively involved in their lives. Especially in the African American families, males are noticeably absent. But increasingly lacking are mothers as well. Children now have members of extended family or social service agencies substituting in the role of parent. This has been caused, not by an unavoidable catastrophe, but by the poor choices made by the mothers. My journey through life has resulted in my being required to live in their culture, the belly of the whale. And the mothers of these children became my new friends while at Glynn County Detention Center (GCDC).

Many of these women seldom mentioned their children. Rather they would spend their time glorifying their life style in the "free world," (drug usage, prostitution, (slinging ass), burglaries, forgeries) or talk about how much time they have "on paper" (probation).

If or when they mentioned the "world of work" or finding a job, their focus was on the most menial positions. They dared to dream. They saw no way of escape from their current economic status. What was most important to them was receiving their "mental medicine and their crazy checks" or their fantasizing their drug usage.

The women at GCDC were unskilled, uneducated and unmotivated. Most of them had been acquainted "from the street" prior to coming to jail. The vast majority of their conversations reminded me of family discussions because they seem to know each other's personal business.

Their daily behaviors consisted of loud, meaningless talk, laughter and more often than not, vulgar language. Some of these ladies would read their Bibles and other religious materials, but would immediately return to behaviors and comments that were contrary to God's teachings. Others spent their time watching television or playing cards. One of the more popular television programs was The Jerry Springer Show. My favorite program was Oprah, but since I was in the minority, I very seldom got an opportunity to watch it. They seemed to think that Oprah was lame and had no desire to watch her show. Many tempers flared during card games so immediately I took Camellia's advise and decided to not play cards under any circumstances.

After being detained at G.C.D.C. for several months, I finally got an opportunity to see Oprah. On this particular show, (I missed the first part of it,) was "a very soft-spoken man" as one of her guests. His name was Dr. Phil and he talked about the fact that everyone experiences some kind of tragedy or unfortunate experience in their lives. The incident was not the thing to focus on but just how you went through the experience was what mattered. That helped me to get a grip on my self. I prayed and asked God to help me to take this lemon (my incarceration) and make lemonade. I had to make sure that something good happened as a result of it!!

Once a week, inmates were given the opportunity to order from the "jail store." Those who had "money on their book" did so while others were given a "care package" which consisted of writing materials, stamps and personal items. The package was often traded for snacks. Each week, the same inmates gave out of food and the begging and bartering for food, even at mealtime, was unbelievable.

While I made every effort to "fit in" with these females, I read Job 11:12 which said, "for an empty-headed man will be wise when a wild donkey's colt is born a man." That confirmed for me that I would never fit. I asked God to help me to survive in a world that was extremely foreign to me, a world that was not my own.

Because I was convinced that God was in charge, early on in this experience, I decided, for my own sanity, to come up with some kind of techniques that would help me cope on a daily basis. Because children and families were so important to me, I decided to use this turn of events to my advantage and learn as much as I could from these ladies while I was in their world. And I began to think that I was "on assignment," very similar to a reporter who had been sent overseas to some foreign country. And although I was sure that I would not be in this situation very long, I decided to learn from it all that I could. It was going to be a test, and I could either make an "A" or an "F." I wanted an "A."

In order for me to accurately learn from these ladies, I had to separate myself from among them. And while I was forced to live "in" their world, I was not "of" their world. So, I started to seriously observe them and took notes during many of our conversations. I had previously met several of the ladies because their children were involved with Hand-in-Hand Counseling Services, Inc. And they were very anxious for me to get out of the detention center and get the agency open again because they and their children needed it. I told them that I felt that God allowed our paths to cross so that I could better serve the loves of my life, their children. The ladies were very supportive and willing to answer any questions asked of them.

One of my initial observations, particularly of the ladies who had an extended addiction to crack cocaine, was what was called their "crack odor." They smelled terrible and the foul odor would fill a room in little or no time. The odor was not offensive to them and they seemed unaware that it even existed. While some of the ladies, after the odor was called to their attention) would take several showers a day, the odor remained because it had entered their blood stream and was being released through their pores, I was told. And it seeped out of their skin. For some, it took up to ten days in jail before the odor was eliminated from their bodies.

Many of the ladies had body odors due to poor hygiene and vaginal infections. At times it was difficult to remain in your room when your "bunkie" changed clothes or passed gas. Yet the detainee with the odor seemed unaware of it. The odor was sheer torture or cruel and unusual punishment.

Another observation that was interesting, yet disappointing to me, was the interaction between younger and older detainees. Absent from the conversation was the wisdom and guidance one might expect from the older lady. Seldom did I overhear an older lady share her experiences with a younger one in an effort to redirect her. Instead their conversations sounded like peers talking to each other. They would simply swap stories, having similar experiences, sex, men, (sometimes women), drugs, violence and designer clothing.

Also prevalent among the ladies was the number who had been sexually molested. At least eighty-five per cent shared their stories of being molested by males and females from age four or six through ages fourteen to sixteen years of age. Later in their lives several had participated in conceptual sex with their molesters, fathers, grandfathers, stepfathers, uncle and even brothers. Most often, this was done to support their drug habits.

I was surprised to see the number of interracial relationships because of the location of the county within the state. It is located in the far southern part of Georgia. During my incarceration at G.C.D.C. approximately ninety-five percent of the white females incarcerated were involved with a black male. And more often than not, her charge was drug related.

Although I would spend hours getting to know the ladies, I also had to spend some time to myself. At times, while in their presence, I thought that I would scream, due to the silliness and trivial, nonsense nature of their conversations. None of the ladies wanted to talk about goal setting, how to become a good parent, building positive self-esteem or budgeting. Those topics were of no interest to them and very few of their topics were of interest to me.

Many times the ladies would have group discussions on how they had "set up" men and robbed them or got away with some other scheme that caused them financial gain. Many of their cons were directed against senior citizens. They were proud of their deeds and looked for new techniques to use on their next victim. They did not seem remorseful and many times would be able to justify their actions. I could only sit and listen because I could not join in their conversation. I simply had not done the same kinds of things and had nothing to add. I was truly a fish out of water. And I started to become extremely uncomfortable in their presence.

I soon started to withdraw to my room and spend hours upon hours reading mostly spiritual or inspirational books. The officers then began to question me as to whether or not anyone was bothering me because I had started to isolate myself. And they seemed concerned that I might try and do something to hurt my self.

But while in the room reading, I would often stop and talk to God about the ladies. I was concerned, not only for their children but also for their lost souls. So when I went out among them, I started to tell them about Jesus. And the more I talked about Him, the more they listened. One day, a lady who was headed to court asked me if I would pray for her because she did not know how. She went to court, the charges against her were dropped and she was released to go home. Some of the ladies called me a witch, while others called me a prayer warrior.

But that was the beginning of my praying for the ladies. While I had difficulty relating to them, I was on familiar territory when it came to Jesus. I had met Him a long time ago and had made HIM the head of my life. I started to feel at home with these ladies because for the first time I determined what topics I was willing to discuss. And I simply refused to have anything to do with negative topics or negative people.

Before I realized what was happening, ladies were scheduling a time to talk with me. They had issues concerning their children and the possible loss of custody as it related to the Department of Family and Children Services. Or they wanted some direction regarding all the particulars on assigning guardianship to family members. I had gained their trust and soon, they were discussing their alcohol and drug addictions and the poor choices they had made in choosing a mate. My room became my office and I began to schedule appointments,

My daily routine consisted of counseling, praying and reading. And before long, I really began to enjoy what I was doing. But every now and then, I would ask God why He allowed me to be locked up for this service. I felt confident that I could accomplish the same things in the "free world." But I guess He knew that I needed to have a "captive audience" for this because I was angry at their apparent neglect of their children. And I let them know exactly how I felt. I was in jail because of my efforts to help their children while they were off doing everything else.

Pretty soon, not only were the officers encouraging other ladies to come talk with me, they began to come themselves. They too had problems with their children or grandchildren, or a family member on drugs or a mate or spouse who just would not do right. And they could be observed gathering in the officer's booth when we formed our nightly prayer circle.

One thing that I did have in common with the other ladies was the desire to be free. I informed them that in Matthew 18:20, Jesus said, " where two or three of you shall agree on earth as touching any thing that you shall ask, it shall be done for you by my Father, who is in heaven." I encouraged the ladies to join me at 9:00 p.m. nightly so that we could join hands in prayer.

At first the participation was irregular but at 9:00 p.m., I would walk in the center of the room and start to sing, what became our theme song, Victory Is Mine. Sometimes I had to stand by myself but would soon be joined by others. The group grew to where eighty-five per cent of the ladies in our POD were participating in the circle. Immediately there was a remarkable decrease in friction and confusion. We ran Satan out of our living quarters.

After about a week or so, one of the ladies from the other POD slipped a note under the dividing door asking if we could move our circle closer to the door, which was a restricted area. They would be on the other side of the door at 9:00 p.m. sharp to join us in prayer and song. Soon approximately eighty-five per cent of the female population at G.C.D.C. joined hands in prayer and song nightly.

I was pleased when several of the officers would request that a certain song be sung. And a couple of the officers lead a song themselves. While we were locked away from society, God had not left us. He was there all of the time. Many, many nights, the Holy Spirit came to visit us and we "had church."

After several weeks of our nightly prayer circle, one of the ladies made flyers and we smuggled them on food trays being returned to the kitchen for the male population on the other side of the building. These flyers invited them to join us (from their POD) and a large group of them joined us as we worshipped. At 9:00 p.m. all over G.C.D.C. the detainees became a mass choir as we sang Amazing Grace. There would be a peace that surpassed all understanding.

Evangelist "Mother" Trottie and her weekly devotions were truly God-sent and became the highlight of my existence during this time. Not only did I attend her services every Thursday night, she would visit me during the day and pray with me and give me words of encouragement. She shared her dream to open a transitional center and we began to work on the goals and objectives for her place, "Life Transformation Center." I solicited the help of my husband to file her incorporation papers with the Secretary of State Office. And her dream began to unfold. We both knew that there was nothing too hard for God and we claimed the victory for the success of her center.

The Sentencing

While in cell 215, at G.C.D.C. (sometimes called "The Potter's House"), waiting to be sentenced, I had two dreams concerning this occasion. Both dreams were very festive, almost a county-fair-like atmosphere. There was excitement and great expectation.

In one dream I saw people coming from all directions, walking towards the courthouse. The numbers were great, and every face I saw I recognized as a friend. Some had even spread blankets on the courthouse lawn and were having a picnic.

The second dream depicted a line of well-wishers and supporters circling the courthouse. They were carrying protest signs and shouting in unison, "Free JoAnn, let her go." Everyone seemed to really be enjoying themselves.

After being incarcerated for one hundred and two days prior to sentencing, I looked forward to the sentencing hearing, regardless of the dreams. I wanted to reunite with my family and pick up the pieces of my broken dreams. My faith in the system had been shattered. I just wanted to go home and hide.

On May 18, 1998, the sky was a bit overcast and the humidity was high. But for me, it was one of the most beautiful days in my life. I was finally going back to court. Mr. Williams had met with me to prepare me for this occasion. We were confident that, if I could be sentenced under "The First Offender Act", I stood an excellent chance of being released and going home with my family.

Camellia and Gloria had lined up a list of very impressive personalities to testify on my behalf at the hearing. While I was in the detention center, they had asked me for names and addresses of friends and supporters. I was able to provide them with this information from the numerous cards and letters (approximately 200) that I had received since my conviction and incarceration.

As the county deputy was driving me to the courthouse for the hearing, I went into a state of shock. People were literally headed to the courthouse from every possible direction. It was just like the dream. Every face I saw, I recognized because they were coming to court for me.

When the car that was transporting me turned into the courthouse parking lot, several of the individuals, Annie Ficklin, Helen Stewart, Charlotte Nash, Kim Dunn and Mrs. Martha Robinson, (friends from my church in Atlanta), headed in our direction. I asked the deputy to please allow me to have some dignity left after this experience, do not allow them to get close enough to this car for them to see me in handcuffs. The deputy sent them in the opposite direction of where he parked the car.

After entering the courthouse through a side entrance, I was taken to a holding cell. My husband, Camellia and Mr. Williams met me in the room and we joined hands in prayer. When the door opened and I was led into the courtroom, it was jammed packed and had people standing around the walls. Looking around, not only was my immediate family in attendance, but also classmates and teachers from my high school in Brunswick. There were members from my church in Atlanta, my former pastor and state representative from Brunswick, Rev. E.C. Tillman, my mentor, Mrs. Winnie Parrish, professional associates and even my co-worker, Betsy Lewis, and God only knows who else! The courtroom was packed!

Mother Trottie had met with my supporters at the courthouse prior to my arrival, and led them in prayer. Everyone was expecting a great more of God and anticipating my immediate release on probation or freed with "time served."

There is a song that Mahalia Jackson used to sing, "Give Me My Flowers, While I yet Live, So That I can See The Beauty They Bring…"

Kim Dunn, a young lady whom I considered "my daughter," took the witness stand and told the judge to release me because she and many other young people needed me back in Atlanta. Mr. Mackford Oliver, my mother's next-door neighbor and member of the local school board, spoke about my being not only genuine but also obsessed and fanatical about working with children. Richard "Pop" Moses, my brother-in-law and friend, said that it was a shame that I had been brought to court in the first place. And when the judge asked my church member and friend, Charlotte Nash, her opinion, Charlotte said, "Jesus dropped the charges."

There were people that I had not seen in quite some time. One of my neighbors from Atlanta and a dear friend, Josephine Smith was there and a cousin from California. All of them could not take the stand to testify, it was just too many of them. But they were there to lend their support and let me know that they cared.

Never in my wildest imagination could I have been prepared for the remarks coming from the individuals who served as character witnesses. The hearing lasted for approximately five hours. A total of thirty-two individuals were called to testify. And what looked to be approximately two hundred people were in the courtroom. Rev. Lonnie McClure, Sr. Director of Christian Education at my church, First Corinth, testified that he trusted me with his life!"

During that entire period as I sat and listened to what others had to say about me and the impact that I had made on their lives, I could only cry and thank God. He had truly answered my prayer. I had always prayed and asked Him to use me to help somebody so that my living would not be in vain.

God used this occasion to show me that my mission had been accomplished. My husband and son took the witness stand and said such nice things about me, including how I put others in front of them. Regardless of my actions, they still understood me, supported me, and loved me. Again, it confirmed that God was in charge.

The prosecution painted an entirely different picture of me. They depicted me as this shrewd, scheming, master manipulator, who had set out to develop this elaborate plot to defraud the state. This included my ability to influence their Medicaid providers to violate the billing procedures, which would place their state licenses in jeopardy, and threaten their livelihood. The prosecution also stated that I had brainwashed my high school teachers and friends into thinking that I was someone I was not. She did not give them credit for being able to think for themselves!

Although my family and friends who had known me all of my life had said positive things about me, and having never been in trouble with the law before this, the prosecutor said they all were brainwashed by me. I was simply a con artist, and the judge believed her.

The judge stated that in all of her years on the bench, (she did not say how many) she had not had an individual appear in her court with the level of education (masters degree) and resources that I had at my disposal. She stated that it was simply impossible for her to believe that I did not know that we were breaking the law by billing Medicaid for counseling services provided by our counselors and not the Medicaid providers.

She further stated that she felt that I was uppity, not humble, and showed no remorse for what I had done. The judge sentenced me under "The First Offender Act" but did not give me the maximum penalty allowed by law, which was ten years on each count. Instead, she sentenced me to ten years to serve five of them in prison and five years on probation.

The courtroom erupted in an uproar. Spectators were shocked! Some stood sobbing while others started yelling. The judge, several times, threatened to clear her courtroom, if order was not restored. In a daze, I stood and told the group that I was o.k. and reminded them that we would always be decent and in order. They quieted down. Then I asked for permission to meet with my son, face-to-face. Permission was granted.

When I left the courtroom, my son met me in the hallway. He ran to me and picked me up and told me how proud he was of me. His smile calmed me down. My son reminded me that this battle was not ours, but the Lord's. He said we only lost this round, but ultimately we would win the war.

That evening when I returned to the detention center, everyone was eating supper. Many of them felt that I would return to the POD to pack my things and go home. Instead, I went back to "The Potter's House" and lay on my bed in total shock. But I did tell God; nevertheless, I am still going to trust You.

Years ago, there was a television program called "This is Your Life." Participants usually had something good to say about the guest of honor. Well, several days after the sentencing, I called and talked to my younger sister, Aundra Green, about the event. She said, "Jo," you got a chance to do something that very few people get to do. "You attended your own funeral and was alive to witness it." Because only then does one say the kind of remarks made about you, when that person is dead and gone and not around to hear it for themselves. She further stated that, "I know that God is using all of this for something and I just want to be a part of it!"

GEORGIA

Medicaid fraud trial to begin

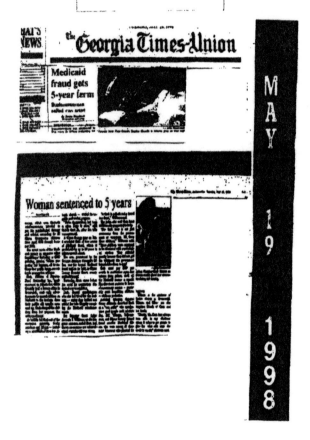

MAY 19 1998

Chapter 3

TRUE TEST OF MY FAITH

Glynn County Detention Center

For two and a half months after my sentencing, I existed at Glynn County Detention Center. My mind had simply shut down; I was on my way to prison. Again the local newspapers and television station informed the community about how this "master-mind con artist" had been dealt with by the Glynn County Court System. I could not believe that all of this was happening to me.

Several of the ladies expressed their anger and disbelief over what was being printed about me in the newspaper. They knew better because they and their children had been involved with Hand-in-Hand Counseling Services, Inc. and had benefited from the services provided. The newspaper and local news broadcast showed pictures of some of the individuals who had testified in court on my behalf. They even included pictures of my church's bus. First Corinth Baptist Church, Rev. E.L. Jones, Pastor, that had been used to transport several of my church members and supporters who came from Atlanta to testify to my character.

I seemed to be moving around in a dazed state. I had very little appetite and was almost unable to sleep. I learned that others were aware of my unbalanced state of mind when the detention center administrator called me to her office. She urged me to sign up to see the mental health person so that

I could have someone to talk to and get put on some kind of medication that would help me to cope with my situation. She further stated that she had read the articles in the newspaper and could easily understand why I might want to hurt my self.

I thanked the administrator for her concern but declined the offer. I informed her that I did not need a mental health person because I had Jesus. Also I assured her that I had no intentions of hurting myself because I was convinced that my faith would bring me through this situation.

I filled my days with reading, taking notes for my book and helping another lady write a proposal for an exercise program, especially since "outside time" was almost non-existent. A structured program, of some kind, would force the ladies to work together with the ultimate goal of getting them to be more respectful towards each other and maintain "peace in the POD."

During the day, whenever out of my room, I was literally surrounded by other ladies asking me for some kind of assistance. Other times, ladies would come to my room to talk with me privately. All I had to offer them was a listening ear, "the truth," and words of encouragement. I kept myself busy so that I would not have time to think about my situation.

Early in my incarceration, I noticed that I was in the minority, because of my age. Many of the ladies readily called me "ma" and referred to themselves as my children. Most of them were conscious of their behavior while in my presence and seldom used profane language around me. And when they "slipped," they were quick to apologize.

One incident I want to share is the time when I had attended church services with Mother Trottie in the library. When we returned to our POD, all of the ladies who did not attend the service had been put on "lock-down" in their rooms because the officers had brought in a lady who was drunk and combative. She had fought with several officers while they were "booking" her into the detention center. Needless to say, for the entire POD to be on "lock-down" status meant that the incident had been pretty bad.

For the previous several weeks, I had the luxury of being assigned to a room by my self. Many days it felt more like an office due to the nature of my interactions with the other ladies. We discussed everything from how to designate custody of their children to how to prepare for a job interview upon their release from the detention center.

Upon entering my room, I was startled to see a pile of linen in the middle of the floor. When I bent down to pick up the linen, I was stunned to see an individual, who looked much more like a male than a female, asleep on the floor. Yes, you guessed it! The combative detainee who had fought with the officers and caused the POD to be placed on "lock-down" was my new roommate.

Immediately I voiced my displeasure and concerns to the officers. They informed me that Jan was a frequent visitor and was very well known at the facility. Because of the past numerous problems she had had with others while in the facility, my room was the best place for her because we were strangers to each other.

I went back to my room unwilling to believe my ears. I asked God just what was really going on! How could He do this to me? He had allowed Satan to set me up to get seriously injured by putting a known violent person in the room with me. At night, we would be locked in that room together, any thing could happen!

As I stood over Jan, looking down at her as she slept, God said to me, "she is one of my children who needs your help." I got mad all over again. I did not work here. And look at the trouble I was in because of my trying to help others. I was sick of it!

It was a violation of the rules to sleep on the floor in the detention center. But the officers had decided to not try and get Jan in her bed because she had been assigned to the top bunk. And she was so drunk they were concerned that she might fall out if she got up there in the bed.

Our rooms are not but so big. Jan was lying in the middle of the floor and it was impossible to maneuver around her. She was even blocking access to the toilet. I just could not live under these conditions.

I made a cup of coffee and returned to the room. The floor was cold and too hard for anyone to call it a bed. I took Jan's pillow, placed it in the floor and sat on it. Then I put her head in my lap and forced her to sip most of the coffee as I introduced myself to her. She needed to have something warm in her stomach.

When the officers learned that I had been able to get Jan to drink most of the coffee, they released the "lock-down" status and the other ladies were able to go back to watching television or playing cards.

I left the room after about an hour and updated the others on Jan's condition. Most of the other ladies knew her quite well and a couple of them expressed concern over my well-being. They knew Jan from the street and they all knew that she also took "mental health medicine."

When I returned to the room to check on my new roommate, I was again surprised to see that she was no longer on the floor. Instead she had made herself comfortable for the night by snuggling up, "cozy as a bug" in my bed. I got mad all over again. But I had to admit that it was kind of funny.

I insisted that the officers issue me some more clean linen. Then I pulled the mattress off the top bunk and covered it with Jan's linen. I woke her up and helped her to get on the mattress that I had pushed under the desk. That position eliminated her being in the middle of the floor and in front of the toilet. I made up my bed with the fresh linen, said my prayers and joined her in sleep.

It should have been no surprise to me that Satan was throwing darts at me. I had to constantly remind myself that I was on strange territory. I had often told the other ladies that being in jail was the same as being "on the devil's playground." And he was not pleased with us singing songs, having Bible studies, and praising God! As a matter of fact, he was down right mad with me. Who did I think I was, encouraging others, telling them that this experience, for most of us, was only a test and that we had a choice to either make an "A' or a "F." And that we could not have a testimony until we had had a test. I tried to encourage many of the other ladies, and even some of the officers, to do what I was doing, having a "faith-walk." Satan was not going to just lie down and let me enjoy myself.

Every day presented some sort of challenge. Being locked away from society with everyone supposedly on equal standing, it seemed that it would be simple to get through a day with little or no stress. Wrong answer! More than ever, I found myself having to rebuke Satan and bind up demonic spirits everyday, all day long.

God was doing a "mighty work" in the lives of many of the ladies at Glynn County Detention Center. He was showing them favor when they went to court and they were being released right and left. Whenever someone was being released, the POD would break out singing our theme song, "Victory is Mine." Usually that song was followed by "Jesus Is On The Main Line (tell Him what you want)." And for many of those who still had to remain locked up, God was cleansing, healing and restoring lives.

Our nightly prayer circle continued to grow and grow. Then one day several of the ladies came to me and asked me if I would help them get to know The Lord. They said that they had been watching me. And now they wanted to have what I had because they were convinced that nothing bothered me. That conversation resulted in our POD holding a mid- day Bible Study, five days a week! God was truly blessing me and I thanked Him. Bit by bit, this environment began to feel more like "my world" than theirs.

But Satan decided that he was going to pull out all of the stops to bring me down and he sent Mary Banks to accomplish his mission. Mary had been in federal prison for the past two years but had been locked up in Glynn County before being sentenced to prison. She had filed an appeal to her conviction and was again being held in the facility pending her hearing.

Many of the ladies knew Mary when she was there before and had helped to care for her because she had recently given birth to a newborn child. Her charges had something to do with money laundering through her numerous businesses in South Carolina. And it was rumored that a couple of the officers at the detention center were somehow personally and financially involved with her. And the interactions between her and them definitely gave the appearance that she was being given preferential treatment.

When Mary was brought back to the facility, she had been assigned to my room but she had to be reassigned due to some type of injury she suffered while in prison. We hit it off right from the start and we had several things in common, mainly being former business owners. But of all the women in the POD, Mary had a real problem with our Bible studies and started to bribe the ladies with "store items" to play cards with her instead of having Bible study and prayer with me.

After a couple of weeks, Mary stopped speaking to me altogether. She started the rumor that I was a witch and was using the prayer circle to cast spells on others. Some of the ladies seemed to believe her and stopped participating in the group. And a couple of nights, I was "in the circle" all by my self.

One day two of " Mary's friends," (my former friends and one of them happen to be her roommate), came to my room to tell me just how much Mary hated me. They said she talked about me all of the time and seemed obsessed with hurting me! They seemed concerned about the intensity of her dislike for me and did not feel that the prayer circle should cause her to be that hostile. And they warned me to be careful whenever I went to take my shower and suggested that I get one of them to watch the shower door to make sure that no one entered without me knowing it.

I thanked them for their concern but made a point to not gossip with them about Mary. I did not want to give them anything that they could take back to her. I had always heard, "he who gossips with you will gossip about you." I told them that I was not worried because I knew that "GOD had my back."

Two days after those two had come to my room to discuss Mary, one of them went to an officer because she had a secret that she could no longer keep. She and Mary had become trustees at the facility and my "friend" did not want to jeopardize her status. After she confided in the officer, their room was searched and the officers found a razor. Mary had hidden it in their light fixture over their sink!

Mary was placed in the "isolation room" on lock down status pending her appearance before the disciplinary committee. The room was located next to mine and Mary became my next-door neighbor. Late at night, through the vent that our room shared, she would sing, Satan is on the main line, tell him what you want. Her song would be followed by some kind of hissing sounds as she called my name, J-o-A-n-n, I'm coming for you! A couple of nights I lay there in my bed, staring at the window, expecting to see a snake at any minute. On those two nights, I was too scared to pray!

On the third day, my next-door neighbor Mary was moved to another POD on the other side of the dividing door. I thanked God! That night approximately eighty-five percent of the ladies again participated in the prayer circle.

About a week after Mary moved to the other side, Carol became my roommate. She too, was a regular at the facility due to her obsession for shoplifting meats from grocery stores. Carol thoroughly enjoyed the challenge of getting the meat from the meat department to the front door of the store. And she told me that she knew that she had been arrested at least fourteen times for the same thing, shoplifting meat.

Carol was a very interesting young lady who shaved her head bald like Isaac Hayes. She had been diagnosed with having at least six different personalities and refused to take her "mental health medicine" because she enjoyed interacting with "her friends" and did not want them to go away. She was proud to let me know that she did not believe in God because He had never done a "d" thing for her.

She was not from Georgia and received no emotional or financial support from family or friends. When it was time to place our order for "store" I would tell her that I would allow her to order a certain amount on my list so that she would not have to do without.

After several weeks of noticing some of my "store" missing, I finally confronted Carol when I had sufficient proof that she had been stealing from me and selling the items to some of her friends. She began to curse me in front of all of the other ladies. I decided that I needed to do something because it felt like she and maybe one or two others thought that they could do me any way they wanted to. After all, to them, I was just "a church lady."

I never got angry to the point of loosing control but I wanted to do something to show her that I was not a "push over." The whole while she cursed, I prayed. I was all right as long as she cursed me from across the room, but as she started to approach me, I picked up a chair and held it over my head as though I was going to hit her. The chair was so heavy that I almost collapsed under its weight.

One of my prayer partners grabbed me and another one grabbed the chair. Another five seconds of me holding that chair over my head and I would have had to set it down and sit in it. It was too heavy and I was worn out. Both of my shoulders ached.

Shortly after the incident, several of the ladies told me that they were not going to let Carol fight me but they saw that I did not need their help. This incident earned me additional respect. I had already earned the respect of the ladies who participated in the circle and now I had the respect of those who did not. But that night I asked God to forgive me for my behavior because I knew that my actions were not pleasing in His sight because I knew that the battle was not mine but His!

Overnight in Pulaski

On the morning of July 28, 1998, I woke up with one thing in mind, to call my brother, James, and wish him a happy 49th birthday. The ladies at G.C.D.C. had had a good morning devotional circle and all was well. I finished helping Kizzie clean her room and fix up herself.

I placed the call to James and we had a very enjoyable conversation. He updated me on his pending federal incarceration for Medicaid fraud (he accepted a plea bargain) and was giving me words of assurance that this was a test of faith for both of us, stressing that our goals had been similar, to improve the quality of life for others.

After our phone conversation, I returned to my room to continue reading a book. I spent a great deal of my time reading, initially to become familiar with different authors and their style of writing but, by this time, I had committed to 'heeding the call' to write a book of my own.

Suddenly my worst fears became a reality. When it was time for one of the ladies to leave the jail, you were headed to one of two destinations. If you heard your name called over the intercom and they said, "pack it up," you knew that you were being released and headed home. If your name was called and they said, "all the way", you knew that you were headed to prison. On July 28, 1998 at 9:20 a.m., the intercom said, "JoAnn Cash, all the way." I was actually going to prison!

Most of the other ladies in the "B" POD with me seemed to be more in shock than I was. Before I could even think, I had to calm some of them down. Several of the ladies started to cry and some were sitting and staring, especially my classmate, Geraldine. Everyone was convinced that for me, things would never go this far. Some of them had children who had been involved with Hand-in-Hand and had been very appreciative of the services provided to them.

It was a bit of a relief to hear that one of the ladies from the "A" POD, Michele was leaving with me. It was a little ironic that we would be traveling together, since we were not speaking. She had helped my former bunkie, Nicole; steal Tender Journey by James P. Gills, M.D., my most favorite book. She was going to prison for violation of her probation because her urine tested positive for drugs.

I locked the door to my cell and completed packing my things to avoid being bombarded with the ladies asking for them. I divided most of my foodstuff and personal items and asked Ruth to share them with the others. The remainder, I designated for Gloria to pick up because I had been informed that I could only have two books in my possession. I chose my Bible and my daily devotional book, <u>Faith To Faith</u>, by Kenneth and Gloria Copeland.

As I headed downstairs to leave the POD, Kizzie and several of the other ladies started to cry out loud. The jail administrator entered the door and said, "Cash, what's the holdup, they are waiting on you." Everything was chaotic but I reminded the ladies to keep the prayer circle intact until each one of them left the jail. And I also reminded them to always trust God. There were tears, even in the eyes of the officers, but not one in mine.

When I reached the lobby of the detention center, I first was told to change from my G.C.D.C. uniform into my street clothes. I was then directed to the same chair that I had sat in several months earlier when I was first booked. I had been held in that facility for 173 days. As I sat there, a white female officer informed me that she would be transporting me to Pulaski State Prison where I would spend the night. I would be transported to Metro State Prison the following day. She also informed me of the travel rules, (no talking, no smoking, no eating, etc.) and proceeded to place me in handcuffs and leg irons. I had never felt more humiliated and alone in my entire life.

Suddenly I remembered my picture of the Cash family back in my cell taped to the bottom of the top bunk. I slept on the bottom bunk and had taped the picture so that I could see my husband and son when I first opened my eyes every morning. I informed the officer that I would like to go back to my cell and get it, and she said "no".

Just at that moment, the door opened and Officer Blind, one of my favorite officers came into the area. She said, "Cash, I think you forgot something," and handed me my picture. Suddenly, I was no longer alone, I had God, whom I could feel and the Cash family that I could see.

After Michelle and I had been placed in the back of the police car, the transporting officer opened the trunk of the car and removed several weapons. She placed them on the front seat beside her, two small guns, a rifle and what looked like a sawed-off machine gun. I closed my eyes to hold back the tears.

We had been riding for about an hour when Michelle and I informed the Officer that we needed to use the restroom. She seemed a bit annoyed but after a while stopped at a convenience store. She got out of the car, after making sure that all doors were locked, and went inside the store to check out the restroom. The officer then took us inside, still in our handcuffs and leg-irons, and we used the restroom.

As we were leaving the store, there were three or four customers at the checkout counter. Once they noticed Michelle and me in our handcuffs and leg-irons, they moved away from us as though we were dangerous criminals. One of those customers was a young black boy, around ten years old. I will never forget the fear that showed on his face.

After returning to my seat in the car, I asked myself, "How in the world did you get to this? You have dedicated your entire life, often at the expense of your own son, to helping children and now they are afraid of you." I did not attempt to hold back my tears. Silently I cried.

After traveling for about two and a half hours, we arrived at what kind of reminded me of a college campus, minus the bared wire, Pulaski State Prison. The transporting officer had to leave her weapons at the front gate and then drove us on to the I.D. section of the prison.

We then had to go into a large room and take off all of our clothes. Next came the shower, no privacy, where we were told to especially wash our hair, underarms, and pubic area with a liquid that was supposed to kill lice. After we had completed this assignment, we were told to enter another room, lean over in front of the officer, squat and cough. Then we had to face the officer, lift our breast and open our mouths. This "strip search" was done to assure that we had not hid any objects or drugs in our bodies. I was so devastated by this procedure until I simply became too numb to pray.

My "street clothing" was exchanged for a white jumpsuit. After we had changed clothes, I was taken to the "lock-down" dorm, where inmates are taken for disciplinary actions and/or isolation.

The dorm reminded me of a huge airplane hangar with different compartments, except, this hangar was made to store women. I walked pass several women who were in the process of stripping wax from the concrete floors and they stopped to stare at me along with all the other women in the area.

I was taken to a cell where I met my "bunkmate" for the night, a middle-aged while female, on her way to Metro State Prison due to violation of her probation. She seemed harmless enough, and I tried to start breathing again.

There were two lockers in our cell, a metal desk and stool and two sheets of steel welded to the wall for our bed. Each bed had a one-inch mattress on it. Sitting on it felt like sitting on bricks, I could not imagine lying down on it to sleep, and we had no pillows.

Later that evening, my bunkie and I were brought two of the most unattractive trays of cold food. The food was served to us through a hole in the cell door. Our meal consisted of some kind of greens, kidney beans, bread and my most disliked meat in the whole world, liver. We also had a bathroom size cup of colored water called tea. I was unable to eat, but I drank the tea.

That night at Pulaski State Prison was the longest night in my entire life. I had to get up and move around every thirty minutes or so, because the bed hurt my body. For a while, I just sat on the floor looking out a window that faced a wide-open area. Several times I considered yelling out the window to try and make someone understand that a terrible mistake had been made. I found myself wishing that the window would somehow stretch so that I could just step out of it and run away.

Around 2:45 a.m., strange noises could be heard coming from the room next to ours. It sounded like someone might be choking and fighting because there were obvious sounds of some kind of struggle. I went to our door and tried to look out of the 5x8 hole in the door. Suddenly a face appeared on the other side of the door and shouted, "get away from this door." It almost scared me to death.

After what seemed like hours of our hearing the noises, several staff finally came to the room next door. We learned that the young lady in that room was having seizures and the noise was her having convulsions. I sat up for the remainder of the night.

We were notified at 5:30 a.m. that "it was wake-up and lights on." There was nothing for us to wash our faces with nor anything to brush our teeth. I wet a piece of toilet tissue to wash my face.

After a cold breakfast of oatmeal, hash brown potatoes, scrambled eggs, biscuits and coffee, I was taken back to the I.D. department. I was loaded into a sixteen-passenger van along with fourteen other females headed to Metro State Prison. Our van was the second of two vans that were being driven by officers with the State of Georgia, Department of Corrections. Overnight, my status had changed from a county detainee to a state prisoner.

As we drove along, I was unprepared for the jovial spirit in the van from some of the ladies, especially those who had been to prison. For them, there was a level of excitement that I had not experienced since my days of returning to college after an extended break, happy to see old friends and new faces. Many of them seemed glad simply to be in the number. The handcuffs and leg-irons did nothing to dampen their spirits.

82

Metro March

Once we reached Metro State Prison, we entered their processing area. There we were assigned to the Diagnostic Dorm and given our specific room assignments, along with the locks to our lockers. We then were issued a pair of black boots, two pairs of panties, two bras, one comb, a toothbrush and toothpaste, a washcloth and a towel and two pairs of socks. The sum of my possessions from "the free-world" was the pair of panties that I was wearing.

Soon after we had been issued our supplies we were taken to an area to begin testing. While we were sitting in a hallway waiting to be tested, any time a staff member or officer walked through the hallway, we had to "stand up in attention." Failure to stand and acknowledge their presence resulted in a loud, rude verbal reminder. On the first day, testing took a total of six hours and we were made to stand at least two hundred times, up and down, up and down.

My bunkmate, Shirley was from Atlanta and lived about ten minutes away from the prison. She and Lisa, who lived directly across the hall, were very helpful in helping me get settled for the night. I was so tired that I had stopped caring. But almost immediately there was a problem. Unfortunately my bed assignment was for a top bunk. Once I was able to climb into the bunk, the height caused dizziness and my blood pressure begin to soar. My first night at Metro State Prison, I slept on the floor.

The days started with a 5:00 a.m. "standing count." Each inmate (as we were referred to) had to stand at attention, by her bed as the officer walked past the room door. Failure to stand up at attention resulted in disciplinary actions; kitchen duty, picking up cigarette butts, extra cleaning or talking to trees (which were non-existence) etc., something degrading and not much fun.

While in Diagnostics, inmates were not allowed to have visitation with their families or receive any items (Bibles, rings, pictures, watches etc.) We were permitted to make ten minutes phone calls. The reading materials available consisted of True Romance Novels. We were allowed fifteen minutes to eat meals. Our wardrobe consisted of two ill-fitting white jumpsuits and a pair of black marching boots. We were counted daily, six times daily.

All inmates in Diagnostics were required to march back and forth to the dining hall and walk in a straight or single file line any time that more than one inmate was present. When approaching an officer, inmates had to say "by your leave" sir or ma'am and wait for permission to be granted before being allowed to continue on your way. You had to stand for however long it took for permission to be granted. Officers often ignored you simply because they could.

My first full day at Metro was spent in the medical unit. During the course of the day one inmate (who arrived with me) Queen, went into labor. Several of us tried to make the staff aware of the situation but all of our pleas seemed to fall on deaf ears. We did the best that we could, trying to time her contractions, etc. This episode ended when Queen gave birth, unassisted to her son in the restroom.

During the first week, inmates were given a "complete" physical. I was able to get a "profile" which resulted in me being assigned to the room with Betty and two others, so that I could have a bottom bunk. This profile also limited the amount of exercise they expected of me, because daily, after breakfast, inmates were expected to participate in the strenuous marching drills and exercises. If you were unable to participate in the exercises, then you had to be involved with the daily dormitory inspections. One was as bad as the other.

From day one, I was simply overwhelmed when I saw the women, approximately nine hundred of them. More than the women, I hurt for the vast number of children, including my son, who were existing without the presence of their mothers.

After about a week of almost freezing conditions, because the air vent was located directly over my bed, I was forced to move to the room next door. Again there were four of us assigned to this room and there was no privacy whatsoever.

The lack of privacy became a major issue for me due to one of my new roommates, who prided herself on being a "stud". Her main enjoyment came in turning out (being the first female to have sex with her) other females. And she had a special interest in older ladies. Believe me I really started praying again.

Sexual relationships amongst the ladies were rampant. Whenever we were allowed to take a short break from the consistent, never ending cleaning chores, the officers would announce, "ladies, go to your rooms, get into your beds, by yourself". That is how they warned you against participating in homosexual activities. But for the most part, it was accepted that this was a natural part of living in prison. The officers really did not want that kind of activity reported to them. They preferred that other inmates just mind their own business. Truth is, some of the officers were participants as well.

On several occasions while cleaning the floors or walls a few of us would start singing a spiritual song. Soon other inmates would join in from all over other parts of the dorm. Occasionally several of us would gather in a room and have prayer. I will never forget this one occasion, while having prayer, the Holy Spirit came to visit and ladies were sobbing and passing out in the floor. Although we were locked away from society, God still came to see about us. We were not forgotten.

On Thursday nights we looked forward to going to chapel services. I will never forget learning the song, "I'm learning to lean and depend on Jesus. He's my friend, He's my guide. I'm learning to lean and depend on Jesus, cause I found out that if I trust Him, He will provide." That song kept me through Diagnostics on many sleepless nights.

This experience provided an opportunity for me to see just how resourceful females can be. Smoking was not allowed in the dormitory however, whenever the inmates wanted to smoke, they would "pop a socket." This was done by taking lead out of a pencil, breaking it into three pieces, and sticking two pieces of lead into each slot in the socket. Then you wrap a piece of toilet tissue around the middle of the third lead. Holding the tissue, they touch the third lead to the other two ends and sparks will catch tissue on fire. Light the cigarette and throw the tissue in the toilet and flush. The other method used to light cigarettes inside the dorm was to get two batteries and two pieces of brillo. Twist the brillo and connect the positive and negative sides and "ground" it to either the locker or doorknob. This will light the cigarette.

It took a little while for me to wise-up to the reason some of the young ladies wanted to borrow my analgesic ointment. It was prescribed for me because of my poor aching shoulder and knees. I learned that they borrowed my ointment to use to disguise the odor when they had sneaked and smoked in their rooms.

During that first week while sitting in medical, I thought I was beginning to lose my mind. I felt certain that I saw Anne Simpson, my former employee, walk pass the lobby window. I was sitting there thinking, "no way" when she walked past the window again. I later learned that she was employed at the prison at a salary of $12,000 less than what I had paid her to run the office at Hand-in-Hand. I thanked God that she did not see me.

The following week, as I was marching with the others to the "chow hall," walking towards me was a very close friend, Yvonne Timmons. She was employed as one of the chaplains at the prison. THANK GOD she did not recognize me as I turned my face to hide from her. Plus, I think she would have gone into shock to see me marching with a "bunch of criminals."

A couple of weeks later, Camellia came to visit. Her visit was allowed, even though I was still in Diagnostics, because she is an attorney. I was in the midst of telling her about seeing Anne when suddenly Anne appeared outside the window of our meeting room. I reminded Camellia that, because of Anne's testimony, she shared the responsibility for my being convicted and in prison. I asked her, why is God allowing Satan to add insult to injury by having Anne see me in a big, white ill-fitting jumpsuit, labeled "State Prisoner."

Camellia and I prayed. She reminded me that, no matter what, "God is FAITHFUL." As I was leaving the visitation area and returning to my dorm, Anne and I met in the doorway. I looked her in the face, spoke to her and smiled. I felt good knowing that God gave me the strength to do it!

About a week following this encounter with Anne, I had a meeting with my counselor. She shared some of her personal experiences with me concerning her involvement with Medicaid. Her ignorance too, could have caused her to wind up right here in prison the same as me. During our meeting, she said that I was very different from the typical inmate and assured me that this experience was just "a test of my faith." She also informed me that Anne had met with the Director of Counseling at the prison and requested that I be transferred to another prison and not be allowed to remain at Metro State Prison due to personal differences she had with me. I prayed to just "let go and let God."

I made a special effort to interact with the different ladies. It was simply incomprehensible for me to understand the dynamics of the female-to-female relationships. In many instances, some of these females opted to stay in prison and "max out" instead of accepting probation. They would prefer to stay in prison with their girlfriend than go home to their children, husbands and families. It was astonishing that the majority of females who were incarcerated are also HIV Positive. Absolutely no precautions are in place to safeguard an inmate who does not have the disease. This environment provides a prime breeding ground for this disease to affect others and spread.

Another interesting aspect of prison life was the number of inmates who were prescribed psychotropic, addicting drugs. Resources needed to deal with psychological issues, for the most part, were non-existent. Therefore, the remedy chosen was to administer a pill at "pill call" and put them to sleep. There is so much excitement in the women headed to pill call that a stranger would almost get the impression that they were headed home! This was simply a way for many of them to escape.

During my 28 days stay at Metro State Prison, I was forced to realize that I was just a number in a system that cared nothing about me as an individual. Prior to incarceration and even in the county detention center, I was referred to as Mrs. Cash, and more often than not, it was said with respect. Metro State Prison called me "inmate," – scum of the earth!

Never in my life had I encountered such harsh, cruel and insensitive treatment. I was forced to sit on the floor for everything except church and chow. No real consideration was given me due to illness, and totally eliminated from the officer's vocabulary were the words "please" and "thank-you."

I read some literature that stated that female inmates, over the age of forty-five, consisted of seven percent of the total female population. Overall there was little respect given older inmates because in most instances they did nothing to earn it. I overheard many conversations between an older inmate giving advice to a child, (age twenty-one and younger). Approximately ninety percent of the time, I was disappointed with and disapproved of the advice being given.

At some point, I had to come to grips with the fact that I had met several young ladies who could easily have been my daughter-in-law. They were attractive, had some intelligence and I believe my son, Calvin, would feel like "they really had it going on." But many of these young ladies were facing if not life sentences, very long prison terms for a variety of violent crimes.

Many of these young ladies had killed a male. I was told that the State of Georgia does not have a "self-defense" law. Even if you are being battered and during the struggle your spouse or boyfriend is killed, odds are that you, the female, will serve some time in prison.

Prisons have begun to offer child nutrition meals and "kiddie" dorms for housing to accommodate the needs of these young, long-term females. Their respect for authority figures is non-existent. They are often ready and willing to try anything because they have nothing to lose.

For Diagnostics inmates, there were very, very limited recreational activities. Your time was spent cleaning, marching, being counted or waiting to be counted. Every night I went to bed exhausted. And many nights I was too tired to sleep!

In Georgia, prisons house females the same way zoos house animals. I believe in a lot of instances, the animals are treated with more respect!

After four weeks in Metro, I began to think, "maybe I am this mastermind criminal that had been portrayed by the courts." While in the midst of this population, most females openly shared, with pride, their criminal activities. Several of them could not believe that they had finally been caught and sent to prison for minor offenses. That was because many of them had committed major crimes and either had not been caught or had found a way to "beat the system."

On the night of August 24, 1998, just before bedtime, Queen braided my hair in some kind of African knots. I had lost a great deal of it due to stress and the lack of care. The majority of the African American females wore braids of some kind. It was a low maintenance hairstyle and hair care products were limited. Inmates in the Diagnostics Unit were not eligible to have their names placed on the waiting list for cosmetology.

That night, after we had been "locked down", an officer came to the room and said, "Cash, bring your stuff to the day room for inventory, you are shipping out." I had mixed emotions, happy in a way because moving on in "the system" meant that I was that much closer to going home. I was sad because, since Atlanta was home for Metro State Prison, and me, I was being taken away from home, family, and friends who were looking forward to visiting me, once I had completed the Diagnostics placement.

On August 25, 1998, I was transported along with thirteen other females to Washington State Prison. Our transporting officer had us handcuffed and shackled, as required by law. But there was a blessing in the midst of the storm. The van radio was turned to 1380 W.A.O.K., the gospel station that I played constantly in my house and car. And during the two and a half-hour ride to prison God came to see about me!

Washington – Valley of Dry Bones

Once we turned off the interstate, headed to Washington State Prison, I no longer could believe that my life was real. I felt as though I was having some kind of out of body experience. Even though I had just left Metro State Prison, I did not feel the real flavor of prison because the Diagnostics Department was separate from the general prison population. Everyone that we came in contact with was just like us, spanking brand new to the prison system, except for the repeaters.

Washington State Prison was located way out in the country. There was nothing in the general vicinity except wide-open space, barbed wire and the prison. And unlike Pulaski, Washington looked like a prison. I had never seen so much barbed wire in my life.

After we arrived we had lunch at little picnic tables outside of the compound but inside the barbed wire area. We then entered the I.D. area and again had to be strip-searched. We also had to remove all braids or plaits from our hair. Several of the ladies attempted to help me loose the African knots from my hair. It seemed that time was of the essence, because we were being rushed to leave the area. We were not able to take my hair down fast enough so one of the officers got me a pair of scissors for me to cut the knots out of my hair. We were photographed and sent to G-2, the Intake Dorm.

Lisa, my Bunkie, a white, twenty-eight year old, was a former schoolteacher and serving time for bank robbery. She was extremely helpful in my transition to the institution. The nicest part of the new setting was, for the first week, we would not have to do much more than sleep. That was a drastic change from Metro State Prison.

The heat was unbearable and the flies, gnats, and bugs were unbelievable. Mattresses were the same size as at the other two facilities, more the thickness of a mattress cover instead of an actual mattress. And the atmosphere felt like you were living in a sweatbox. There was no air conditioning and at 11:00 p.m. the room was ninety-five degrees. I felt like a person in shock, just going with the flow.

On the following morning, while sitting in the dining hall, I was again overwhelmed when I saw the number of females incarcerated at this facility. I simply could not stop thinking about the number of children affected, including my son. I sat at the table with three other ladies and they began to tell me that everything was going to be all right, just trust God. I was unaware of the tears that had fallen into my food. One of the ladies at the table became a close and trusted friend, Winnie Williams.

The weather was like an inferno... and the bugs, gnats, flies and mosquitoes were absolutely everywhere. Bugs were in the food and in the bed. They either flew or crawled in your eyes, your mouth and your nose. The compound had no trees and very little grass, but the bugs seemed to appear like magic. I thought, "this is a valley of dry-bones."

The Intake Dorm (G-2) was full of activity, mainly because it was constantly in transition. It received new arrivals weekly, either Tuesday or Thursday from Metro State Prison. That is where every female that was new to the prison system had to enter before becoming a part of the general population at any of Georgia's three prisons for females. And transfers from the other two prisons also were housed in G-2 initially, before being assigned to another dorm on the compound. It was absolutely heartbreaking to see the ease at which the majority of these females adjusted to this setting. Young women with extremely lengthy sentences often appeared to be arriving at "summer camp" with lots of laughter and the highest level of excitement.

This environment was a lot less stressful than Metro. Inmates were not required to stop when approaching all officers, only those with advanced rank. The constant cleaning of the dorms and having to stand for all counts was not required. I was actually able to catch up on my sleep, even with the tremendous heat and unusually loud noise level.

After a week, I was enrolled in Substance Abuse 101, a requirement for all new arrivals, and assigned to the laundry detail. This course was taught by one of the inmates, Judy, who was serving a life sentence for murder. During this period, I just tried to stay focused on the fact that any day now, I would be delivered from this setting.

After two weeks in the Intake Dorm, I went to work in the laundry. I was one of eight females on this detail and we were responsible for the daily washing of clothes for approximately eight hundred females.

Having to go dorm to dorm to pick up and deliver clothes, regardless of the weather and push those laundry carts was some of the most strenuous work I had ever attempted. The only advantage to this detail was that it gave me access to both yards of the prison because the compound was divided into "the east side" and "the west side." Ordinarily, inmates were only allowed access to the yard where their dorm was located.

Lisa, my Bunkie, was moved to the dorm next door and my new roommate was Christie, an eighteen year old white female, who had been sentenced to thirty years for robbery and aggravated assault against an elderly man. She did not actually commit the crime but was present when her boyfriend did it. He had not yet gone to trial (while she sat in prison), was out on bond and had gotten a new girlfriend. Immediately, she decided to get her a girlfriend.

I remained on the laundry detail for approximately three months before the Medical Department recommended something different. The amount of standing required, as well as the wear and tear on my body, started to affect my health. Also, during this period, I lose nine pounds. The detail was so exhausting that often I returned to the dorm and fell asleep in my clothes.

"Yard-call" was the most popular activity in the institution. This provided an opportunity for inmates to "socialize" with their friends, but more accurately, meet their lovers. Smoking and courting were the most favorite past-times. Some days the ladies would play volleyball, basketball, jump rope or play with a Frisbee. Playing cards was the second most popular activity but that was confined to the "day room" and not allowed outdoors. But I honored the promise that I had made to Camellia while I was in the county jail, and did not play cards at all no matter who asked me to do so.

My new detail was " light duty" in the kitchen where meals were prepared daily for over one thousand individuals. Cooking was also done for a male prison located directly behind our facility. This detail required sweeping the floors in the kitchen and wiping down the appliances after breakfast.

After mid-day count and lunch, I, along with Eddie Wilson, a late fifties African American, went back to the kitchen. She had been incarcerated for twelve years for killing her abusive common-law husband. We were responsible for cleaning the coolers used to store and deliver the "pack-out" lunches. These lunches were for inmates, male and female, whose details did not permit them to eat in the chow hall at lunch. They were like the "carry-out" lunches.

It was during this time that I was moved to Dorm E-2, a dorm for older inmates and those with medical conditions. It was a nice chance from G-2, quiet and laid back. But of the sixty-six females in the dorm, thirty-one of them were serving life sentences for killing either their mother, husband, child, family member or boyfriend. And the majority of these ladies had been in prison for some time. I could tell that they were very suspicious of my behavior, my speaking with a friendly smile and showing genuine concern for them. And I did not know just what I was doing either! I was praying and trusting that God would not put more on me than I could bear.

Each day the remains of the pack-out lunches were returned to the back dock and thrown away in large, black garbage cans. This was also where all of the food from the kitchen and garbage from all of the dormitories on the compound was delivered. The trash detail collected the trash and took it away. We then had to empty and wash coolers and then wash and stack garbage cans. Once that was complete, we had to scrub the cement dock.

Two days a week, I had to work the evening detail alone. Eddie's schedule gave her two evenings off in addition to weekends. Mine only allowed for me to be off on Saturday and Sunday. But that was a blessing in disguise.

Many days I stood in the midst of garbage, with the temperature hovering around twenty degrees and the water from the hose freezing as soon as it hit the cement. I often reminded God of His promises. He said, if you are faithful over a few things, then I will make you a ruler over many. I said, "God, You know that I have a "Masters Degree". You also know that I have written to the counseling department, the school department and the parenting department, asking to be assigned to a detail so that my skills could be utilized while I am here. But You allowed them to put me in the midst of garbage. Well, O.K., if that's the way You want it! I am still going to glorify You! I'll just make this dock and these garbage cans shine like new, and that is exactly what I did!

Many days some of the officers would stop and talk with me as I cleaned up garbage. They could not understand how I could be singing and praising God in the midst of such a mess. I would tell them what my son Calvin, constantly told me to remember, this joy that I have, the world didn't give it and the world can't take it away.

The prison allowed inmates to receive food items in their Christmas packages. That was the only opportunity to receive your special "treat" (holiday nuts, individually wrapped candies or packaged cookies). And the package could weigh up to twenty pounds. Shortly before Thanksgiving, I wrote my best friend, Annie Ficklin, ("Fick"), and made her aware that many of the ladies would not receive treats for the holidays. And I asked her to solicit the help of some of my other friends to send packages for twelve ladies whose names and EF numbers I had collected.

My friends, "Fick," Rosetta Mindingall, Shelia Moore, Helen Stewart and one of my beauticians, Linda Hines (Bold and Beautiful Salon), made me feel so proud. They sent twelve of the "most desired" packages to arrive at Washington State Prison to ladies that they did not even know. Of the twelve ladies, seven of them had not received a Christmas package in the past five years.

I enjoyed my Christmas package containing many of my holiday favorites. It was an extra blessing to me because my son made the selections and sent it to me.

It was almost earth shattering to realize that I would be in prison for Christmas. Mary Lester, who had been in prison for sixteen years for killing one of her newborn twins, asked me to "direct" the dorm's Christmas choir for the institution's Christmas Program. I told her that one of my life long dreams was to direct a choir. And I thanked her for the opportunity. At the time of the invitation, I was unaware that our performance would take place in front of approximately one thousand inmates and staff. Needless to say, the "E-2 Sounds of Joy" were a hit in the program, with our black robes and sequenced banners. The choir consisted of about twenty murders, aggravated assaulters, kidnappers, robbers, and drug dealers, and they were now my family. I often asked the question, "God, how on earth did this happen?" These ladies had committed some horrible crimes and here I was, trying to help others. These ladies were very suspicious of me and seemed unaccustomed to any one showing them any kindness without some hidden motive for doing so.

About two weeks before Christmas, God put it on my heart to not be around anyone who was hungry on Christmas Day, especially since the institution only served two meals and no lunch on holidays and weekends. Many of these ladies no longer received much financial support, if any, from their families partly because of the length of time that they had been incarcerated. The other reason was because many of them had caused some real serious damage to their families' relationships before being locked up. For many of their families, the old saying was true, "out of sight, out of mind!"

I was continuously supported by my family and friends and had about three hundred dollars on my account at Washington State Prison. God laid it on my heart to feed the dorm on Christmas Day.

After some careful observations and consideration, I solicited the help of several ladies to work on different committees. I needed them either to make coffee, tea, noodles (soups), dip, or cut up pickles or sausage or find large garbage bags to use as tablecloths or to locate backs from legal pads so that we could decorate them and use them for serving trays. All of the food items for the dinner were purchased by me and stored in the lockers of different committee members. They did not believe, at first, that I trusted them that much! I took great pleasure in watching the ladies work together and forget their problems and just focus on the dorm dinner.

My enjoyment came in seeing the mission accomplished. I did not eat one bite! Just to watch the ladies work together and serve each other and put their differences aside, made it a good Christmas for me.

Another one of the lifers, Pricilla, was asked to lead us in prayer. At the time that I asked her to do so, I don't think she had spoken to me, but I did not care. Pricilla asked the ladies to join hands and form a circle, and lead us in a beautiful prayer. Tears filled my eyes when I saw that approximately ninety-five percent of the ladies in the dorm were also in the circle and ate Christmas dinner at no cost to them.

On New Year's Eve, 1998, Eddie and I walked towards the back gate and the men's unit to collect coolers as we did daily as part of our detail. Both of us were a little depressed being in prison and we were just trying to uplift each other's spirits. Neither of us felt very well; her legs were hurting and my back was bothering me. But we were trying to make it to collect the coolers so that we could go to our dorms and go to bed.

We approached the gate that separated the men's unit from the women's, because often some of the coolers were left there for us to collect and wash. That gate also led to "the free world." The gate officer failed to come out and acknowledge our presence, so Eddie and I turned around and limped on towards our dorms. She lived on the West side of the compound and I lived on the East side. Barbed wire and several gates and fences separated the two sides.

When crossing the yard and heading towards my dorm, I knew something "big" was going on. Everywhere I looked, I could see officers running while talking on their portable radios. As I approached the dorm, my cousin, Joelynn, (whose incarceration led to my meeting Mr. Williams) said, "girl what have you been up to?" Your name is all on the radio! I did not know what on earth she was talking about and I walked on to the dorm.

As I entered E-2, to sign in, the dorm officer said, "Cash, where the hell have you been?"...stand your ass over there (indicating to the side of the other ladies who were signing in), until I can talk with you. Inmates ALWAYS had to sign in at the desk with the officer-in-charge, whenever they entered or left the dorm.

Once she finished signing the others in, the officer explained to me that the security camera had identified me and another female at the back gate. It had been radioed to each officer all over the compound that Washington State Prison had two inmates attempting an escape!

At first, it was very funny to me, because they did not realize the pain that Eddie and I were experiencing. We could barely walk, much less run away. But when several of the administrators entered the dorm to question my actions, it was no longer funny!

No one had informed Eddie or me that the warden had allowed the back gate officers to leave early because of the holiday. The entire area where we worked had been designated off-limits to inmates. But no one told us! After listening to much ranting and raving about what could have happened, they finally excused my behavior.

That night I asked several of the other ladies to join me in watching Bishop T.D. Jakes on the Trinity Broadcasting Network (T.B.N.) television station. All my adult life, with the exception of only a couple of years, had been spent in church for a "Watch Night" Service. And I was not going to be denied that experience because of my present environment. Bishop T.D. Jakes sermon, prior to midnight, established the right atmosphere for several of us to go down together on our knees, in the T.V. room, and we thanked God for sparing our lives to see another year.

Throughout my incarceration I had friends write and ask what they needed to do in order to come and visit me. It was difficult enough for my husband and son, so I decided that since I would not be here for very long, I would just "tuff it out" and not let any of my friends have the nightmare of seeing me behind all of this barbed wire. So I would not tell them the procedure for scheduling a visit to the prison, nor did I complete the necessary paperwork for them to do so.

I received a true blessing on January 2, 1999, with a special visit from my closest friends, Annie Ficklin, Shelia Moore, Rosetta Mindingall, Helen Stewart and Camellia, one of my attorneys, who coordinated the visitation. The visit lasted from 11:00 a.m. until 3:00 p.m. and it was wonderful. There were very few tears shed and they each brought plenty of quarters so that I could buy anything my heart desired from the vending machines to eat during the visit. They had words of inspiration and displayed overwhelming support. I had forgotten that I had friends that were genuine in their belief in me.

It was then that I told God that I was renewed in my belief that I was in prison because this was just an assignment and a true test of my faith. I was not here because I was a bad person. I asked God to use me, even if it meant that I would have to remain, for a while, at Washington State Prison.

I also made the decision to not allow any more visitations, other than my husband and son. While this visit with my friends had been "just what the doctor ordered," I was not willing to subject them to the level of pain that they experienced. Yes, they said all of the right things and their behavior was appropriate. But nothing could disguise the pain that I saw in each of their faces when it was time for them to leave the prison knowing that I would be left behind. To see their hurt broke my heart.

I was told that James Peacock, Ms. Beddington's grandson, had made two attempts to visit with me. He was not on my visitation list and had caused quite a disturbance when the officers failed to believe that he was my son. Several of the officers made me aware of this white man coming to prison visitation claiming to be my child.

Several weeks later, my roommate, Marsha, helped me to organize a Super Bowl Party. There was added excitement for those of us who were sports fans because the Atlanta Falcons were playing in the game. Marsha, however, was a fan of the opposing team.

For the game, we divided the tables with fans for each team and sat up refreshments. We also made a few banners and had some cheerleaders. Although the Falcons were not victorious, the ladies enjoyed themselves because, for most of them, this was their first super bowl party. And it very well was the first one for the prison as well.

Every day offered a new experience for me and I seemed to move through life in a fog. I did not feel like "a prisoner" and I guess I did not act like one either. It was not unusual at all for an officer to call me to the side and ask, "Cash, what are you doing in prison, you just don't seem like you belong!" I would respond that I just came to hang out with them for a while.

My work detail changed from the kitchen and garbage cans to a teacher's aide in the GSAMS (customer service)/GED Program. I enjoyed interacting with the ladies and motivating them to work towards their GED. On several different occasions my students would come up to me after class and say, "Ms. Cash, if you had been my teacher, I never would have dropped out of school!"

During "yard call" I walked and talked with a couple of the ladies who had similar interests as mine. I wrote a "Needs Assessment Questionnaire" and had approximately one hundred and fifty copies distributed throughout the prison. After we had about seventy completed copies returned, we wrote a proposal, Liaison for Inmates Needing Knowledge, (L.I.N.K.), a program designed to foster communication between female inmates and the "free world."

Shortly after we completed the proposal, I was selected as one of the inmates to move into the "honor dorm." My new roommate appointed herself as my campaign manager and I was elected "honor dorm representative to the Warden's Office." I was also selected to become a part of the Praise Team and a Prayer Warrior for the Chaplain's Department. It was also an honor to be chosen to participate in the thirteen weeks Experiencing God Bible Study. I thanked God because no longer was I just surviving, I was thriving. God had truly shown up and showed out!

It was approaching the time when I would be eligible for release from prison after serving one-third of my sentence. It started to become very difficult to stay focused and remain positive because I wanted to go home. And I was very anxious to hear when I would be released.

I had spent the past month without a roommate and it had started to feel like I was living in a suite having a room by myself. I had been able to really devote quality time to my Bible studies. And I was expecting a miracle from God. Needless to say I was blindsided when I was informed that I would have to move into the dreaded "drug dorm" and complete the twelve weeks Prison Substance Abuse Program (P.S.A.P), even though I had no history of drug abuse.

Shortly after I entered Washington State Prison I would often hear many of the ladies talk about the drug program and I was really impressed with what they had to say about it. I thought to myself, this program really sounds great. It is just a shame that the ladies had to come to prison to be exposed to it. As an administrator, I was very interested in the curriculum.

I asked my counselor to allow me to participate in the program and she said "no"! My records made no mention of my having a substance abuse problem and therefore I was not eligible for the program. And there was a very long waiting list of addicts who needed the program before they would be considered eligible for parole.

My having to enroll in a drug program after being told that I could not came as a complete shock, when I had been anticipating my release, was almost enough to shatter my faith and I almost gave up. Then I remembered the poem about Footprints, when I could not walk, God would carry me. And I just let go and let God. He was there to carry me every step of the way.

Bobbie, my little Mexican roommate, was a joy. She and I had some wonderful times in our room studying "The Word." I helped her with her reading and she helped me to learn our PSAP theme that we all had to memorize and recite before we could graduate from the program. Bobbie shared with me how she had become an alcoholic at age nine and would often have to drive her alcoholic mother home during that time. She never really had a typical childhood.

One day while we were talking in the room, Bobbie said, "Ms. Cash, I know why God sent you to prison." She said, "He knew that you would be here and you would teach me what a real mother's love feels like so that I can be a good mother to my son, Eric." I cried!

Living in the midst of former addicts was the most difficult part of the entire incarceration. They seemed to march to the beat of a different drummer. Many of them continued to "fanaticize the drug" and the acts they had committed to get their drug of choice were unbelievable. But I gained a much better understanding of addiction and even some respect for some of them.

When it was time for us to graduate from PSAP, I was selected to serve as Mistress of Ceremony for our graduation program. But I looked forward to moving back into the Honor Dorm. The following week, I was asked to remain in "the drug dorm" and serve as a peer counselor. I accepted the challenge.

After a couple of months, I really began to have second thoughts about my housing situation. The constant loud noise and combative nature of many of the ladies was more than I could handle. And after I witnessed one of my former roommates, (who was serving a life sentence for stabbing her boyfriend to death) beat another inmate in the head with her lock, that she had put her in sock, I requested that I be returned to my placement in the honor dorm.

It was less stressful in the honor dorm but while I was away, things had changed a great deal. A new dorm rep. had been elected and there were many new faces. My new roommate was a lady who actively practiced witchcraft. She had served twelve years of a life sentence for her part in a devil worship sacrifice. There were evil spirits in the room and for the first two nights, I was unable to sleep.

That following day, after my roommate when to work on her detail, I prayed over my oil and anointed our entire room asking God to run anything out that did not belong. Two days later, my roommate asked to be moved to another room. I thanked God!

Once again, my work detail was changed to that of Education Orderly. I was now expected to work in the department mopping and buffing the floors, sweeping and dusting. For a moment or two, I was insulted. Then I remembered that God was in charge and He knew what He was doing. I decided that I would sweep the sidewalk outside the education department because no one else ever wanted to do it. That gave me an opportunity to see ladies from both yards because everyone had to pass the education department regardless to where they were headed. My broom and I had a ball!

The previous year I had been recommended but had to be placed on the waiting list for Kairos, a prestigious three day retreat that was sponsored by Christian ladies who lived in the "free world". They give up their time and money to come into the prisons to spread the love of Jesus Christ. All of the ladies who were chosen to attend Kairos were envied by all of those who were not chosen for it. To my surprise, I was chosen for Kairos #7 at Washington State Prison. I sat at the table of "Martha." That three-day experience was almost worth having to come to prison to experience. It literally changed my entire life.

The love displayed by that group of ladies from the "free world" was what true Christians are supposed to have for each other. And one of the most memorable activities during Kairos was the Forgiveness Ceremony. It was that activity that helped me to achieve one of my biggest goals.

Throughout this incarceration, I wanted to be able to leave whatever scares, hurt and damage done behind me. I wanted to leave it all in prison and not take any of that extra baggage with me when I left. This was just an assignment, and assignments do come to an end. My prayer had become, God please do not let me leave here "smelling like smoke!" Kairos helped me be able to forgive. God knows what we need even before we realize that we need it.

As my second New Year's Eve approached, I again prepared to celebrate with a Watch Night Service in the Honor Dorm. Once again I was able to participate in a service and Bishop T.D. Jakes was instrumental in eliminating our fears about whatever was happening, "in the real world" with the Y2K madness. We again thanked God for sparing our lives and prayed that our families would be safe.

It did not seem that a whole year had passed since I had my visit with my friends. Yes, I was approaching another birthday and there were days that I just walked around the yard with my radio earphones and allowed

Bishop T.D. Jakes and his choir to reassure me that this was only a test, this assignment that I was on. But oh how I wanted it to come to an end.

Visitations and phone calls were very strained with my husband and son. They were busy doing their own things and I simply was no longer a part of it. But the time had finally come for me to hear something from Mr. Williams, my attorney, regarding the status of my appeal. He had received $850 from a fundraiser that had been spearheaded by my girlfriend, Shelia Moore, to help offset the cost of any legal matters.

Based upon my understanding, Mr. Williams had been to court a couple of times and had filed several motions. But all I knew for sure was that I was still in prison. I also knew that I had to have a copy of my transcript in order to be able to file an appeal to my conviction.

My husband and I had discussed the issue of the transcript on several occasions. He stated that "the law" dictated that the judge had to give me a free copy of my transcript because I no longer had a source of income due to my incarceration and could now be eligible to receive it because of my "pauper status." My position was, if the judge does not give me a free transcript, go on and pay for it. I did not see a problem with that because I had authorized him to get the money from my teacher's retirement with the school system. So the money should not be a problem.

Mr. Williams had informed me that the cost of the transcript would be $5,000 and because I had money in my retirement, the judge felt that I was not eligible for a free copy from Glynn County. When I informed my husband that the transcript had to be paid for, he informed me that he had spent the retirement money on helping him catch up our bills. My husband informed me that he borrowed $2,100 from his brother and sent it to the attorney. He said that that was the best that he could do. I learned that getting my transcript and securing my freedom had not made his "list of things to do," while he had the retirement money.

I then came face to face with my true worth to my husband and our marriage of twenty plus years. I begged him to do whatever he had to in order to come up with the money, otherwise I would have to go back to Glynn County and face the same judge who had sentenced me, as a beggar. I pleaded with him to save me that disgrace! The hearing was scheduled for Friday, January 14, 2000, the day after my birthday.

I asked God just where He had intended to draw the line? Just how much more punishment was I going to have to bear! I told Him that I would just settle down and stay in prison at Washington, but please, please do not let me have to go back to Glynn County Detention Center in Brunswick, Georgia.

Chapter 4

WHEN THE HURT HITS HOME

It is difficult to recall exactly when, during the course of my journey, that I began to notice disappointments from home. I had been adamant about not wanting my son to see me while I was in the detention center in Brunswick. The newness of and the unbelievable events happening to me resulted in an enormous amount of mail and financial support.

On July 4, 1998, I allowed my son to visit one time while at that facility. My husband had been there about three or four times. After all, they lived three hundred miles away. But during the course of the five and a half months that I was incarcerated in Brunswick, neither my husband nor my son sent me one dime. In fact, I asked them not to. It was not a problem because I was blessed with the maximum amount allowed ($100.00) on my account.

During the period of time (28 days) that I spent at Metro State Prison, visitations were not allowed for inmates who were in Diagnostics. Being in Atlanta made me feel better because I was closer to my family and my friends. But being there hurt too, because I was so far away. I was closer to them but in another world.

Once I arrived at Washington State Prison, confident that I would only be there for a very short period of time, I was determined that I would "tough it out" and not have any visitors, especially my family. The appearance of the facility, with the dreary looking buildings and the massive amounts of barbed wire were terrifying to me and I wanted to spare others that experience.

After several months of trying to "go it alone," I discovered that I needed to see my family more than I needed to spare them the experience. By this time, I had really begun to become concerned about my own mental stability. I got to the point where I could not pray. And I felt that I had to see my husband and son and hold them in order to stay alive.

Although that first visit was both joyous and painful, it gave me the strength I needed to persevere. One of the first things that I noticed was my son's tremendous weight loss. He and his dad assured me that they were eating meals properly and that he had just gotten taller.

Shortly after their first visit, they each agreed that they would come and visit me anytime I wanted them to do so. They were willing to do whatever necessary to help me hold on in my present environment. I told them that I did not want them to visit often, but whenever I felt that "need" for them, I would give them a call. And they assured me that they would come whenever I called them.

I had been at Washington a couple of months when Calvin informed me that he had received my retirement check for my twenty-three years with the school system. I still had money on my account at the prison that was being sent by my two sisters, friends and supporters. Calvin was to use my retirement of $42,000 to pay off my outstanding bills, estimated to be between $12,000 and $15,000, use a portion to help him maintain our household and to put the balance in a savings account.

Calvin's receipt of my retirement check was devastating because it caused a realization that I could no longer deny. This experience was no longer a nightmare, it was a reality. My career with the school system, with all of my hopes and dreams had truly come to an abrupt halt. It was over. And that day, my spirit died. But at the same time, I knew, deep down, for me to be experiencing all of this, God had a better plan for my life.

None of the Cash's are great letter writers, although the ones that I had received, especially from my son, will be cherished for a lifetime. I called home at least once a week, but on a few occasions, maybe as many as three times a week. But that was very rare. We maintained consistent communication, usually Sunday mornings. But after a while, my husband began making little comments about the phone bill.

While in prison, inmates are allowed to receive monthly, pre-approved packages. I asked Gloria to send the first one because she was in possession of my gold chain and cross, wedding band and earrings. I had left them in Brunswick, in her care because jewelry was not allowed in the county detention center. She also sent me a watch along with some other personal items.

Three months after receiving my first package, I asked my husband and son to send the second one. While it contained my request for more personal items, make-up and my favorite cologne, I felt that it might be a little awkward, but fun, for the guys to pick out nail polish and eye shadow for me. I stressed my request for my cologne. While I realized that it was a little expensive, over $50.00, I wanted the same scent I had prior to incarceration. That was the only way that I could maintain my individuality. Because otherwise, I had to dress in a uniform and look like everyone else. And this had been the cologne that I had worn exclusively for the past four or five years. I loved it!

My guys did a great job with the items selected for my package. I was more than pleased with the make-up, eye shadow, foundation, lipstick and nail polish. They sent a bottle of nail polish remover, but it was not allowed. But I was on cloud nine. It was just after Christmas and before my birthday (January 13th), and I felt so much better wearing my cologne and smelling like me. They sent it in the crème form because cologne sprays are not allowed. And I had not ever purchased it in the crème before and did not know that it was a little bit more expensive than the spray.

When I called home to say "thank-you" for my package, my husband immediately began to complain about the cost of the cologne. He had never purchased it for me before I was incarcerated. And he wanted to know why I needed "to walk around prison" wearing such expensive cologne.

A short time later during one of our Sunday morning conversations, when my husband and son were pledging their support, we agreed that they would come and visit once per month. They assured me that it would be no problem especially since neither of them worked on weekends.

Because I was less than the best at responding to letters, after a while my mail and financial support became a trickle. It became increasingly difficult to write to others and tell them that I was doing well when I was not. I wanted to be at home.

With the decline in the financial support that had been provided by others, it became necessary for me to call home and ask for money to purchase my personal items and small weekly treats from the inmate store. After my initial request, my husband sent money every two weeks for several months.

Then his supply all but dried up. Because my son was still living at home and working full time, I began to request that he send money. He would assure me that it was no problem. But after not receiving the money as promised, when I would call to inquire about it, he would say that he thought his dad had sent some.

I assured him that if his dad had been sending money, then I would not be asking him for it. And even if his dad was sending money, I was old enough and responsible enough to receive money from both of them at the same time.

The monthly visitations stopped occurring as well. My son started to work at another drug store on weekends and my husband was "busy." Several times they had promised to visit and did not do so. After hours of being dressed and waiting for them, once I faced the fact that they were not coming, I would go to bed, wanting to die from the pain. During this period, whenever my husband or son did send me a money order, there was no letter or card or any communication. When I received my mail, it consisted of an empty envelope indicating the amount of money that had been sent.

I was devastated due to the way I was being treated. It felt like they had adjusted to life without me and I was a "problem" for them. It began to feel like my relationship with them was somehow based on money. And they were the same two whom I had often given my last dime. This was the most devastating pain of it all, because this pain hit home. There was only one thing that I could be assured of and that was God. Because His word said that He would neither leave me nor forsake me. And because I believed that, I held on!

Back Where I Started

GLYNN COUNTY DETENTION CENTER - I was transported from Washington State Prison on my birthday, January 13, 2000, back to Brunswick, my hometown and my nightmare. Before leaving the prison, the ladies had been very kind to me, giving me cards, gifts, a beautiful new Bible and "licks." My cousin, Joelynn, while working on her detail in security, overheard a call that said officers were on their way to the prison to pick up someone for Glynn County. And she had a feeling that that call was about me. So instead of being pressured to "pack-up" immediately, I had approximately two hours to prepare to leave. Once again, God had shown me favor. And I thanked Him. When it was time to leave my dorm, three of the ladies assisted me in taking my possessions to the property room. Even the Glynn County officers helped me to inventory my belongings.

Since I was scheduled to be gone only overnight, all of my personal items were left in the property room at the prison. The only thing that I was allowed to take with me was my Bible. The officers realized, after we had traveled some distance away from the prison, that they had forgotten to get my medication for my blood pressure and my hormone pills. After they apologized for doing so, I told them that I understood why they forgot my medication. They were focused on the six guns, their protection from me, that they had to collect when leaving the prison. After all, first things first, I was a dangerous felon! But when they stopped at the store to buy gas, they offered to buy a snack for me. I declined!

During the ride to Brunswick, I talked to God a good bit. I told Him that I was numb, and simply did not understand why He was allowing this additional humiliation of my having to return to the jail in Brunswick. But I also submitted, because by now, I realized that none of this was about me, but the path that He had chosen for me. That He was in charge. That this was just another part of "my test" and I was still determined, no matter what, to make "an A." After all, I had put all of my hope and trust in Him.

I arrived at G.C.D.C. at approximately 4:45 p.m. and called Gloria to ask if she could get me something to wear to court the following day. If not, I would have to wear some of "the court's clothes" because my prison uniform had been exchanged for a county uniform. I was still in "booking" at 8:00 p.m. when I was informed that Gloria and another friend Julia "Netta" Bryant, had dropped off clothes for me to wear to court. The judge did not like "county detainees" to wear jail clothes to her courtroom. The officer-in-charge had granted special permission for the clothing to be accepted. She then told me that she would put me in a room by myself. That too was a blessing. Soon afterwards, I saw five or six officers who remembered me from my stay before I was sent to prison. And they were very nice to me.

After I was processed into the detention center, I called home. I told my husband and son that I had been handcuffed and shackled on my birthday. And the experience was most painful. I also told them, that at this time, my spirits were too low to pray. If my prayers already prayed could not carry me through this event, then I was not going to make it! My son then prayed! He also told me that the following morning, he would resume taking some college courses. I told him that he had just given me the strength to hang on.

As I entered the living quarters (A POD), there came a sudden hush over the area. Mrs. Cash was yelled from six or seven different mouths at the same time. They treated me like I was a super-star. I immediately recognized several of the ladies who were there with me before I was sent to prison, and some others who later said that they had heard about me. I felt like I was "back home." And I could recognize Kizzie's voice calling me from the other POD.

Much later that evening, Mr. Williams spent about an hour with me trying to prepare me for court the following day. He informed me that I needed approximately $5,000 to obtain a copy of my transcript. I thank God for good friends, because shortly after my incarceration, one of my life long friends, Sheila Moore, along with Camellia Moore, started a support group to assist me with my legal expenses. They had raised approximately $850 and forwarded it to Mr. Williams' office. My husband had sent $2,100 that had been loaned to him by his brother, John Cash and his wife, Gloria, for a total of $2,950 but that was not enough to get the transcript. We would be asking the court for the difference of $2,050 under "Pauper Status."

During the course of our meeting, Mr. Williams tried to anticipate the kinds of questions that would be asked of me by the judge and the prosecutor. I asked him the question, once we file this "appeal" would we win and MY NAME be cleared?" He stated that he believed so, and went on to explain his interpretation of the law to support it.

One of my mother's favorite sayings was, "God always has a ram in the bush," meaning He always makes a way of escape or works out a situation. That ram, on this particular morning, came in the form of the Judge's bailiff, who had been assigned to take me to court. She was someone who knew "of my story" and was very kind, considerate, and the sweetest spirit.

Mr. Williams had informed me that the court's calendar was real hectic and warned that I should be prepared for a long day of waiting. About five minutes after I entered the "holding cell" I began to give words of encouragement to the other young lady waiting with me because she was facing some very serious charges along with her boyfriend (who was old enough to be her father). Then she told me that she felt that the Lord had sent me back to Brunswick to talk with her because some of the other ladies had told her about me.

I prayed with her and soon afterwards the officer who had brought me to court appeared and gave me some perfume crème to wear. And then she brought me a cup of the judge's coffee. The new pants suit brought by Gloria as well as the coffee were perfect for waiting in the cold holding cell. It was a nice surprise because after about one hour of waiting, I was called into court.

When I entered the courtroom, the first thing I noticed was the facial appearances of the judge and the prosecutor. They looked bad! Their lives seemed to have been much more stressful than mine. I immediately prayed and asked God to have mercy on them. I had spent the last two years hating them and now I could feel nothing but pity.

The courtroom was crowded, but unlike my last court appearance, I saw no familiar faces. My testimony to the fact that my husband had betrayed my trust in the manner in which he spent my retirement money and not paid for my transcript that was vital to my clearing my name was painful but truthful. I felt confident that both our parents and our friends would have been hurt and disappointed to hear my "yes" and "no" answers to some very painful questions from both Mr. Williams and the prosecution. Even though, deep down, I wanted to believe that my husband felt that I was owed a "free" copy of my transcript AND would get one, I was both ashamed and embarrassed to have to speak out against him. After all, this was my husband of twenty-nine years.

Once again, the judge refused to believe me. She felt that I was continuing to try and "get over" on the state. She informed me that Mr. Williams had been assigned as my "court-appointed" attorney for my appeal (which he had not told me) and that was more than what the state should do for me after what I had done.

The judge's final ruling was that, since my retirement check was in excess of $42,000, I would have to "prove to the court" my efforts in pursuing criminal charges against my husband "BEFORE" she would agree to grant me "pauper status" and give me a free copy of my transcript. The motion was denied!

As I was leaving the courtroom, I began to thank God for His presence in speaking for me during my sworn testimony. And yea thou I walked through the valley...I feared no evil. I knew He was with me, because I felt Him! To have to endure this very, very painful but necessary experience reminded me of the day when "we laid mother to rest." The experience was painful but necessary!

When the Bailiff came to take me back to jail she said, "girl, God is already moving." The judge has ordered that you be held here in Glynn County for ten days before you go back to prison. In ten days, anything can happen, including you going home, so you just keep on praying. I was returned to the jail in time for lunch!

The ladies in the POD were so very nice to me, giving me coffee, socks and panties. I started to think that the ten days away from Washington State Prison, with these ladies, would not be bad especially since a couple of them had asked if we could start our prayer circle again. Less than an hour after that request was made, things changed!

Satan was not about to allow me to go unchallenged in "his territory." Out of the blue, an officer announced, "Cash, pack it up, you are moving!" I whispered a prayer and gathered my belongings. Several of the ladies came to my room to offer their assistance. They were very distraught that I had been told to move to the other POD. But before I left their area, I hugged each one, strangers included, and encouraged them to keep their heads up and always trust God. I also reminded them that their being in jail was "only a test of their faith" and reminded them that we each had a choice as to the final grade we earned, an "A" or an "F." I assured them that my final grade would be an "A."

When I reached the other POD, I was happy to see four ladies that I knew very well from my first stay at that facility, including Faye, who had been in Diagnostics at Metro during the time I was there. Again it was a great relief to not have to live with total strangers. And Kizzie gave me the biggest hug of them all.

My room assignment was 110 and as I entered the room, I was surprised to learn that I had been assigned to a top bunk. Washington State Prison had issued me "a medical profile" for a bottom bunk due to the problems I was having with my blood pressure and stiffness in my legs and shoulders. I had also been taking an antihistamine for my sinuses that also helped me to sleep.

I would be really taking a chance on getting injured due to a possible fall by trying to sleep on a top bunk. And besides, there was no ladder to climb to reach the top bunk. I made the POD officer aware of the situation but decided to go on and make up my bed so that it would not be said that I refused to comply with instructions. But I told the Lord that this needed His intervention.

At the time of my arrival all of the rooms had only one "detainee" per room and each of them was sleeping on a bottom bunk. And no one seemed willing to move to a top bunk nor did I expect anyone to do so. In a place like this, it was a luxury to have a room by yourself. The shift supervisor sent me word that he would see what he could do tomorrow but that was my room for the night! I asked permission to pull my mattress down on the floor so that I could sleep safely. Permission was denied and I prayed some more.

I was real sleepy because I had been up all day and had been given the medicine for my sinuses. I laid my pillow on the desk and sat on the desk stool and tried to sleep. The "bunkie" assigned to the room had been at the detention center for several months and had never had a roommate. She had just had major surgery and had to take a laxative three times a day. She was nice enough but it was obvious that she did not want nor need a roommate.

After waiting about two hours, I was assigned to the bottom bunk in room 208, the same room I had when they moved me to this POD a little more than eighteen months ago. The young lady already in the room asked to move next door to room with a girl about her age. Now I had a room all to myself. I thanked God!

For the next six weeks, Glynn County Detention Center would once again become my home. During this period, several memorable events occurred and God showed up time and time again. He provided everything that I needed when I needed it!

Mr. Williams met with me and explained an affidavit he had drawn up that would satisfy the court as to my attempts to recover a portion of my retirement money from my husband. I told God that I would pursue any and all avenues to obtain my transcript because it was vital in my efforts to clear my name. I reminded Him that He was in charge, and if He would have me in court against my husband, then so be it! I signed the affidavit and told God that only He could stop this from going any further. He then instructed me to have Mr. Williams "hold" the affidavit until further notice.

My long-standing best friend, Annie Ficklin, approached my church, First Corinth Baptist and others and raised the remaining $2,100 needed to pay for my transcript. She had been there for me throughout the existence of Hand-in-Hand and believed in me 150 percent. Her efforts resulted in my not being forced to file suit against my husband. Again God worked through one of His angels and showed me favor.

Instead of overnight, as expected, I remained at G.C.D.C. approximately six weeks before I was returned to Washington State Prison. This stay was an absolute nightmare. And many times Satan tried to convince me that he had won and was now in charge of my life.

Although incarcerated, Washington was sorely missed. There I could at least move around, going from my dorm to my detail and then to the dining hall, on a daily basis. Also I could attend church services several times a week as well as go to the library. While at G.C.D.C., movement was limited to leaving your individual room and going into the "day room" or T.V. room. We were allowed to attend weekly church service on Thursday nights with Mother Trottie. I was blessed to leave the area weekly for my visitations with Gloria and Marion Moses, my sister-in-law. Although neither of them was in good health, they were there to see me regardless to how they were feeling. They came to lift my spirits. And that they did! Very seldom were we taken outside for our recreation period, they said because of their shortage of staff. Like several of the ladies that I had met when I was here before, I could not wait to get back to prison.

Because of the lack of structured activities, Satan reigned supreme. Days were stressful, spent filled with gossip, backbiting and depression. Not only were we locked up, but many days locked down (confined to our rooms) as well, due to Kizzie's acting out behaviors.

I asked God why He had brought me back to this place. And He responded, "there is work to be done here." The following day Kizzie asked if I would start our prayer circle again like we had before. She was on lock-down and I asked some of the ladies to join with me outside her door. I remembered her favorite song, Shake the Devil Off. We sang her song, I led the group in prayer and Kizzie cried and asked God to forgive her of her sins. That was the beginning of our nightly prayer circle.

Different ladies came and went, but the prayer circle lasted throughout the duration of my stay. I constantly reminded the ladies that the circle was not about me. That it was their responsibility to keep the circle going and pray for each other whether I was there or not. And several of them made a commitment to do so.

111

After many, many days of reading, waiting and praying, the officers finally called me to pack up. I was finally being taken back to prison. Many of the ladies and the officers hated to see me go. But I was more than ready to move on through this journey and see what else God had in store for me. And because my good days had outweighed my bad days, I was still going to trust Him.

During the trip back to prison, the transporting officers lost their way due to construction on the highway. They pulled to the side of the road to study their map and regain their bearing. After several minutes, they still were unsure of the directions. From the back seat of the police car, I began to give them verbal directions back to the prison. One of the officers asked me if I could show them directions on the map and I answered "yes" and proceeded to point out the directions to them. We all were surprised when it was noticed that my hand was free of the handcuffs. I just slid it out when they asked for my assistance! Immediately their error was corrected. After all, I could not be trusted! But they followed my directions back to the prison.

When I returned from Brunswick, my detail changed from GSAMS Aide to Education Department Orderly. While I had more formal education than the staff, and all the other inmates assigned to that department, I was assigned to sweep, mop and buff floors. For the next month, I spent two hours each day in the mornings and an hour in the afternoon sweeping the sidewalk outside the department that allowed me access to both yards in the prison. I had an opportunity to meet and greet all of my friends. It was a blessing in disguise.

I settled back into my routine in the Honor Dorm. While I enjoyed having more time in the dorm to work on writing this book, I really missed helping the ladies work towards their G.E.D. When not writing, I was reading books to help me to make it through the day. I also had been asked by the Chaplain Department to assist them in working with the young ladies assigned to the Boot Camp, which was located directly behind the prison. I attended church at every opportunity and was just waiting on God to deliver me. I no longer had a roommate, and life (for prison) was good.

It was unusual for me to fall asleep as early as I did, but I woke up to the prison announcing "lights out and lock down." I jumped up and hurriedly put my dirty uniform in the T.V. room with the others to be washed. As I headed back to my room, the officer called me and said, "Cash, I am not supposed to tell you but we are shipping you out tonight." I had been back in prison for about six weeks. I went into shock because the only place that I wanted to go was home. She told me that she had no additional information but that I needed to get ready to inventory all of my belongings.

I went to my room and just sat on my bed. I did not question God. I was just too weak. But I promised Him that wherever He led me, I would go. I stopped and wrote the dormitory a goodbye letter and hung it on the bulletin board. I began by saying, dear ladies; the time has come for me to depart. I reminded them that our incarceration was only a test of our faith. We each had a choice in this test to either make an "A" or an "F". I also reminded them that yes, we are our sister's keeper and it was our duty, as Christians, to look out for each other. I promised them that I would be back, some day to see them and told them that I would keep them in my prayers. I woke my cousin, Joelynn and made her aware of what had happened. She was as stunned as I and we cried together. It really hurt me because I found her in prison, and now I was having to leave her there. I left many of my snacks and personal items with her and encouraged her to keep her head held high and continue to trust God.

After I completed my inventory and packing, I was escorted out of the dormitory and to the chow hall to eat breakfast. I had an opportunity to say "good-bye" to Bobbie, my former bunkie who was working in the kitchen. As I was handcuffed and shackled and led to the prison van, I promised myself that I would not look back. I didn't. I remembered what happened to Lott's wife. I did not want to be turned into a pillar of salt. I just asked God to come on and go with me wherever I was headed. By now, I was assured that He was in charge and whatever He said goes. It was He who had orchestrated this move to another place on my journey back to where I started.

The High Cost of Transition

The State of Georgia has two transitional centers for females, one opened in November, 1975 in Atlanta and another, which opened during the month of October, 1999 in Savannah. The criteria for selection at either of these facilities is nebulous, at best, but hundreds of women anxiously await an opportunity to leave prison and go to "The House," as they are commonly called. These are <u>work release programs</u> for the State of Georgia, Department of Corrections.

At the start of my incarceration, the only "house" in existence was the one in the Atlanta area, Metro Transitional Center. Both of my sisters, along with my husband, encouraged me to make application to be sent to "the house." But I wanted no part of it. This was due primarily to the fact that the program's superintendent was none other than one of my "little sisters" from college, as well as a former member of the same social club, The Sensuous Ladies, as my two sisters. I was determined to save myself from the embarrassment of facing Nancy, the Superintendent, as one of "her girls." I never made any request whatsoever to be considered for placement at "The House."

On March 23, 2000 at around 11:30 a.m., I arrived at Metro Transitional Center. I had many mixed feelings about coming to this program, however on the trip to "The House," I decided that I would do whatever I had to do in order to get "out of the system." It was then that I reminded God of His promise to never leave nor forsake me!

Once I arrived, I was immediately impressed with the lack of barbed wire at the facility. And after several days, I appreciated the fact that I was in that program "by choice" and could easily walk away at any time, if I chose to do so. And many of the "residents" as we were called, (no more inmate) wore regular, "free-world" clothes, and left the program to go to work everyday, and get PAID. That was very appealing to me. They were women, just like me, many of them I had met behind the barbed wire fence, in prison

New residents were housed in the "B" Building and were required to wear prison khakis (pants and shirts) for the first four or five weeks of orientation or until they were classified and received work release status. Residents were assigned three to a room with two lockers that had to be shared, often with known thieves, if one happened to be your "bunkie" or roommate. And none of the rooms had a door. Small screens were provided for privacy to change clothes in the room and it was required that panties and bras be worn at all times.

There was very little tolerance for roommate disagreements or what the administration referred to as "prison mentality." It was stressed that if one could not get along at "The House," then one was not ready for "the real world." Hitting or physical touch was not allowed, without exceptions. Homosexual activity was a violation that resulted in immediate return to prison. Women also were not allowed to hug each other, to comb another's hair nor arch another's eyebrows. This behavior resulted in a Disciplinary Report (DR) being filed against the residents involved. Each DR cost $4.00 and could result in a resident being assigned extra duties, having work or "pass" privileges taken or being sent back across the street to Metro State Prison, which is almost located in "The Houses" back yard. It served as a constant reminder of where we had come from.

Many days I simply stared across the street, remembering the horror of being behind all of that barbed wire, and thanking God for delivering me. My heart would break daily when I could hear the women, in Diagnostics, struggling to endure the morning exercise drills or their footsteps as they marched to and from chow. I hurt because they hurt. I knew their pain because I once was one of them. And for me, Sundays were the worst. Can you imagine being in prison on a Sunday morning? That was almost unbearable!

"The House" was blessed to have a variety of churches and organizations to come in and "minister" to the ladies. But none was better than the services provided by Elder James Murphy and his wife, Edwinett. Their message could hold me from one month to the next.

Each day began with breakfast around 4:45a.m. And very similar to Diagnostics, the days and some nights were filled with "details," (cleaning, cleaning and more cleaning). Whatever the maintenance needs of "The House," the chores were performed by designated residents, supervised by "long-term maintenance" residents who were residents not eligible for work release status because of the amount of "time" that was left on their sentences.

The goals of the program at the transitional center were exactly what was needed for "typical" woman leaving prison. It was designed to gradually assist them with the skills necessary for a successful transition back into society. The program afforded participants an opportunity to address personal issues that were "medicated" and otherwise ignored during their incarceration – self-esteem, battered women, anger management, Alcoholic Anonymous, Narcotics

Anonymous, parenting, GED preparation, and The World of Work. Overall, "The House" provided an opportunity for residents to "make an honest living" by being placed on jobs and assisted with budgeting, prioritizing, and saving their earnings. Each resident had her wages mailed by the employer directly to "The House", where she was required to pay up to 30% of her weekly salary for rent.

The typical resident is a female who had limited education, and needed much structure and support. She had very poor self-esteem and had experienced few, if any, successes in her life. Her outlook on life was dim and she had no real concept of a goal-oriented future. More often than not the typical resident was also one who had a history of substance abuse and some physical/sexual abuse as well. She had also given birth to several children but had not been an effective parent to any of them. This female had no more than six to eight months remaining prior to her temporary release date from the Department of Corrections.

"The House" places the residents in a position where they are forced to get a job and walks them through the process. It also enhances their self-confidence and lets them know that they have nothing to fear. The program helps residents establish good work habits, offering "a hand up instead of a hand-out." Upon completion of the program, each resident should have saved a couple thousand dollars to help them get started again.

Fortunately or unfortunately for me, I was not a "typical resident" and had more education, training and experiences than the majority of the staff. I had extreme difficulty with the inconsistencies and the rational used by the staff in their interpretation of the rules. In many instances, the rules changed with the shift officers. And trying to survive the average day there was much more stressful than an average day in prison! At least the rules were consistent, for the most part.

Many of the staff members, right from the start, had problems with me for what seemed like no reason at all. Some would say things like, "oh, here's our queen" or "you think you got it like that" or "you ain't running nothing here!" While I put forth a great deal of effort to fit in, most of the time, I stuck out like a fish out of water. Many of the rules made no sense and I had some difficulty going along with dumb things. As a result, I received two D.R.s and several infractions. However, when I noticed the impact of "me" getting into trouble and what it did to several of the young ladies and especially my son (when one of my passes home was revoked), I was able to survive the foolishness.

My two "bunkies" welcomed me to the "B" Building. While one was beautiful, both spiritually and physically, the other was not. She was a full-fledged lesbian, unlike the majority of females in prison who participated in homosexuality for a variety of reasons. This "bunkie" would climb over the wall at night into the next room to spend some time with her girlfriend. One morning around 3:00 a.m., I awoke to find our next-door neighbor leaving my "bunkie's" bed. Later that morning, I asked that roommate, if the neighbor had been discovered, who would get the D.R., all of the residents who lived in the room or the one who had the visitor? I told her if I ever saw our next door neighbor in our room again (and I also told the neighbor) that I would ask my counselor just who would be liable for that behavior. They freaked!

It was sometime during the month of April 2000, shortly after I arrived at the transitional center, that I learned from Camellia the status of my transcript. She had placed a call to the Clerk of the Court in Glynn County because I had been unable to make contact with Mr. Williams to find out if he had received it. As of January 23, 2000, he had received a total of $5,000 to pay for it.

The Clerk informed Camellia that she really had not begun to type my transcript because she had been assigned two death penalty cases. Those cases took priority over all others. She further stated that she would not begin work on my transcript until she received full payment for it because only recently had she been paid half or $2,500 I was shocked!

For several months my attempts to reach Mr. Williams failed. Messages were left at his office by Gloria, Camellia and me, but to no avail. There was no response. Mr. Gresham wrote him a letter, not as my attorney, but as my friend, requesting that he contact me. But seemingly that letter was ignored as well.

Once again my trust had been violated. I believed that Mr. Williams would do what he had agreed to, what he had been paid to do. Although throughout my incarceration, I had met several ladies, including Marsha, one of my "bunkies" at Washington State Prison, who had very negative comments about his negligence in his representation of her. I thought to myself, "no way." Not again! I had put my trust in him. Foolish of me because the Bible tells us to put our trust in no man! Obviously I had not learned a thing!

One day while thinking back over my life since my indictment, I started to laugh and just could not stop. For the first time, my words to others suddenly took on new meaning for me. For real, this was nothing but a test.

I just could not believe the darts Satan had thrown my way in an effort to shatter my faith. Once again I reminded him that he was nothing but a "bear-faced" liar. I was going to earn an "A" and not an "F." Yea, I was going to continue to trust God no matter what!

In the meantime I would continue on my journey called "living." I realized that I could determine the quality of my journey because the battle truly was not mine. I knew that God would deliver me from the hands of my enemies. I felt confident because I knew that if God could turn a staff into a snake, then surely He could deliver me and clear my name. I know that, with Him, justice delayed is not justice denied!

"Classification was the process that prepared residents to return to the "real" world. It was the four or five weeks period of time that was used to get residents familiar with the expectations of "The House" and the work release program. We all knew that to leave the program without permission would result in an escape charge being filed against us. Also an additional one to five years would be added to our sentence. Classes and/or groups were held every day, almost all day. And when you were not in a structured learning situation, that time was spent performing "details." And that included outdoor details of cutting grass, washing prison vans, sweeping the parking lots and picking dandelions.

My most enjoyable experience at "The House" coincided with my completion of the classification process. It was my participation and graduation from Mr. Ed Menifee's World of Work Program, sponsored by the State Bar of Georgia. The program was designed to help females transition into the world of work particularly if they were interested in owning their own business.

The members of the class voted to wear black and white. All of the residents were at the transitional center directly from prison and many had absolutely no family support whatsoever. Partly because I was "at home" but mainly because I am blessed, it was not difficult for me to get the things that I needed. But many of the residents were from all over the state and not as fortunate as me. My dear friend, "Fick" made sure that I had my black skirt and white blouse.

I was selected to go to the "Thrift Store" to locate black and white pants, skirts and blouses for the members of the class in need of those colors. My selection was due, in part, to the fact that I had completed classification and just had not gone to work yet and some of the other residents were working and unable to shop for themselves.

We were successful in getting the colors and having all the residents dressed in black and white for the occasion. My husband, son, "Fick", and another close friend, Phyl Macon, attended as my guests. And the program was a tremendous success. Most residents participating in the program were shocked because all of the practices leading up to the actual graduation had been messy and chaotic. Satan had had a field day. But once again, the prayers of the righteous made the victory possible!

On May 6, 2000, I was allowed my first six hours pass from Metro Transitional Center. It was the first time I had been inside my house in the past twenty-seven months. The surroundings were very different than what I had left behind. A new subdivision had been built in my neighborhood and even my yard had been planted with a variety of greenery.

Once inside of my house, I was unprepared to see "the state of things." Everything was exactly where I had left them two years ago! Two days before Camellia and I flew to Brunswick, January 31, 1998, to my Change of Venue Hearing, my husband had given me a bouquet of flowers. They were beautiful. I placed them in a vase on my table in my living room. Almost two and a half years later, they were still there!

From the intensity of dust seen everywhere, the house looked like it had been abandoned. I estimated that ninety-five per cent of the items were still in the same place as two years ago. From appearances, my husband and son had simply made "a path" to move back and forth through the house. It became obvious that they had not lived there, but merely existed in my absence. They had not truly gone on with their lives without me, as I had often accused. But instead, they went to prison with me! I was devastated because I could now see the level of hurt that they had endured.

Every room was the same, including my bathroom, which had the same guest towels hanging in it. My son had told me, while I was still in prison, that right after I was incarcerated he began to sleep with my favorite pillow because it smelled like me. It was still there on his bed. My husband had brought my luggage and clothes from Gloria's house in Brunswick. All three pieces remained packed and the contents undisturbed.

No maintenance had been done to the house. The exterior trimming badly needed painting and there were numerous leaks in the ceiling. Pots or bowls were simply put in needed places to catch the rain, including right inside the front door in the living room. The front door no longer opened properly because the wood floor under the carpet had swollen due to it remaining wet for extended periods of time.

During that first pass home, my husband cooked dinner and he, our son and I sat at our kitchen table for our meal. My husband blessed our food but before the end of the meal, I prayed and thanked God for bringing me back to my family and to my house, Also, I thanked Him because, "He heard my cry."

My husband gave me a bouquet of flowers, he said, "to go along with the old bouquet. Instead, I threw the old one away. When I asked my son why items in the house had not been moved, he said, " Mom, I did not want you to come home and have to look for anything. Me and daddy thought leaving things as they were would make things easier for you." I cried!

After I had become eligible for employment, I was told to not take just any job but to wait on a job that would use my skills and pay for them. I was also informed immediately that "The House" would not allow residents to work with children. I was devastated because for the past almost thirty years, children had been my life.

I noticed that the typical jobs obtained through "The House" were geared towards the typical resident such as clerical, maid service and fast foods. However I looked forward to being allowed to work, regardless of the job or the pay. While I was given an opportunity to visit the Georgia Department of Labor to find a job on my own, staff at "The House" was not even considering me for one of "their" jobs.

I had interviewed for a job in customer service where my roommate, Robin, was employed at Federal Stamp and Seal Company (FESSCO). She had also "unofficially" set up this opportunity for me. My interview with Michael Lawler went well but the company decided not to hire me because I was adamant about my reopening the counseling center upon my release from the traditional center. They did not see me as a worthwhile investment to train me to do the job and then I leave the company in a matter of months.

It was later that same day following my interview, on a Wednesday, that my counselor, Mrs. Sapp, the "head" counselor, by the way, broke the news to me. "Since I had deliberately sabotaged my interview by stating my intentions to reopen my counseling center, if I did not have a job by that following Monday, "The House" would send me back to prison." She further stated, "you said the wrong thing; honesty was not always the best policy." I was shocked for two reasons. First, "The House" had made absolutely no effort to place me on one of "their" jobs and the second reason was, I was not a liar. If I were going to tell a lie, it would have been when the prosecution offered me a six months sentence and two years probation to say that I deliberately set up a fraudulent scheme with Medicaid. That was a lie and I would not tell it. It would possibly have saved me two years in prison.

I asked my counselor for permission to use her telephone and placed a call to Elnora Gordley, whose agency, Brown-Glover Business Group, Inc. had been the accountant for Hand-in-Hand Counseling Services, Inc. Once I explained my dilemma, she asked, "How much do you have to make, because your going back to prison is out of the question." And she scheduled to interview me the following day.

While I had access to her phone (regular daily phone privileges started at 4:00 p.m), I called Robin at work. I informed her of my situation and she "went to bat" for me with Michael Lawler who in turn "went to bat" for me with the owners of the company.

After I returned from my interview with my former accountant, who offered me a position with her company, I learned that FESSCO had called "The House." They had informed Ms. Mapleton, "The House's" employment counselor that they had reconsidered their decision and wanted me to start work on that Monday, the same day I had been threatened with returning to prison. God intervened, once more, because now I had been offered two jobs.

I accepted the job at FESSCO, in its Typesetting Department, because it was the better decision, at the time. Elnora's office was located in the same office complex as Hand-in-Hand and almost within walking distance of "my" house. I remembered the rules and felt that the temptation was too great for me to not try and go home, considering the amount of time that I had been away. It felt too good and I heard my mother's voice say, "everything that glitters ain't gold!" However, I will always be grateful to my friend, Elnora, who was willing to do "whatever she had to" in order to keep me out of prison. The salary at FESSCO's was the smallest hourly wage I had ever earned, with its time clock, scheduled breaks, and an overall insensitivity to the needs of its employees. But I knew that if I was faithful over a few things, God would make me a ruler over many.

My ten-hour passes from the transitional center were limited to my home and back to the center. But I desperately wanted to have my hair permed by my real beautician, Cheryl Drake at By Appointment Only Salon before I started to work. When I called Cheryl and told her that I wanted to have my hair permed but had no more than forty-five minutes to get the entire process completed, she said, "come on." I explained to Cheryl that after one hour from the time I left the transitional center, an officer could call my house to make sure that I was where I was supposed to be. If the call was made and I was not at the phone, I could be returned to prison. Cheryl said we could get my hair done in the allotted time.

When I arrived at the salon, several of the ladies that I knew before going to prison were there for their scheduled appointments. Our reunion was enjoyable but they were on pins and needles, not wanting me to get in trouble. They allowed me to go ahead of them.

Once I left the salon with my new perm looking like only Cheryl could do it, I headed home. And when the officer called my house, I answered the phone.

My immediate supervisor, Jonnie Lazzara proved to be a blessing. And because of her and Mike Lawler, I worked harder than I had worked in a long time. It was important to me that I did a good job for them.

Once I started working, "survival" was the name of the game with my daily routine at "The House." I would have to get up around 4:30 a.m. and catch a 5:54 a.m. MARTA bus (public transportation was the only means of transportation allowed) to the M.L. King Memorial Train Station. I would then ride the train to the Georgia State Station and then catch my bus, (#1 Coronet) on to work. My roundtrip from "The House" to work was three hours daily. And my return time was 6:18 p.m. unless I worked overtime, which I sometimes did.

Riding MARTA was indeed a new experience for me. More often than not, I tried to disassociate myself from the other ladies from the transitional center. First of all, I was ashamed of the fact that I lived at the center. And secondly, the behavior of the ladies (overall) was disgusting. Loud conversations held with mostly men about their time in prison, with little remorse, was the usual topic. And it was generally followed by sexual talk that was extremely inappropriate for public transportation.

I tried to hide in the crowd and not be "one of them" because it was commonly known that there were some convicts riding that bus. But the general public just did not know exactly who they were.

It was impossible to hide because some young lady was always calling me "Ma" or attempting to get me to sit with them on the bus. Their behavior was appropriate with me sitting next to them and I often passed around my copy of Our Daily Bread in an effort to keep them quiet.

Once I reached downtown, I had to transfer to another bus. That bus transported approximately eight women and fifty men to the industrial area where my office was located. Conversations were very different from the ones I had become accustomed to hearing after being in prison with women. There were very few "gentlemen" riding the bus and if the bus was full when I got on, no one would be eager to offer his seat to me. Instead they would talk about how tired they were from the day before and why they were not offering their seat.

One morning, on our way to work, as the bus attempted to drive up a hill, it simply stopped. The bus driver did not say a word, but I later learned that it had happened so much in the past that the riders automatically knew what to do. I got off the bus with everyone else. The driver started the bus and we all walked up the hill behind it. By the time I reached the bus, I was too tired to lift my legs to step back on it. After yelling at me that I was going to make everyone late for work, three men dragged me in the back door to the nearest seat. I thought that I was having a heart attack. That is what caused me to have a conversation with one of the ladies on the bus, Eula.

That evening on the return trip home I was still trying to believe that I had actually paid to ride the bus but because it stopped, I had to get off the bus and walk up a hill behind it. With no refund on my fare! I asked Eula, who was several years older than me, if we had in fact had to get off the bus and walk up the hill behind it. She said that she had been on public transportation all of her life and she was thinking that maybe she was just "caught up in the moment." She said she was so tired that when she got to work, she had to go in the restroom and lay down on the floor before she could do any work.

After several weeks of working, I was moved to the "A" Building at the transitional center. This building housed only working residents and long-term maintenance residents. It was an incentive, earning the privilege of moving there because that meant, while there were still three residents per room, the room had a door, walls (instead of a petition) and I would have my very own locker. After moving in, it was amazing the difference a door and wall made. I got my first "real sleep" since I left prison.

It was during this time that I had to face my current situation with my new friends who rode on MARTA. Eula rode the second bus with me and had not seen me on the bus with any of the ladies from the transitional center. However, Eula's co-worker, Sylvia, lived a short distance from the center and was on that first bus with me and the other residents.

One morning Sylvia and I were talking as we waited at the Georgia State Station to catch our second bus. She said, "I told Eula that you be on that bus talking with all them convicts. And Eula said maybe you were one of them. I told her no, that you probably worked with them as their counselor."

I confessed to Sylvia that she was right in that I did counsel with the ladies. But I was also "one of them." She started to stutter, turned and almost walked into the side of the building. Several days later I joked with them about their comments. I told Reginald about what happened and we all had a great big laugh about it.

Both of my new "bunkies" had an extensive history with "the law." One had been in prison before and the other had been in and out of jail for the past ten or so years. They had shared room 141 several months before I moved in and in spite of their efforts, I still felt like an outsider.

It was a plus for me that we were not strangers. Carol Lawrence and I had developed a relationship based upon our attending the religious services offered at "The House." We also were two of the residents given an opportunity to attend Bishop T.D. Jakes' "Woman Thou Are Loose Conference." Like me, Carol was attempting to live the life of a true Christian. Mattie, the other roommate, and I had known each other at Washington. We both were in the PSAP Program at the same time, we lived in the same dorm and she was one of my students while I worked as an aide in the GED Program.

Maybe it was because I knew that "my journey" was almost over that started to catch up with me. It was extremely difficult to live in the room with these two ladies. If one of them was at work or on pass, it was a bit more bearable. But when the three of us were "at home," it seemed to be an evil spirit lurking in the room. And I felt depressed a lot of the time. I had problems accepting the fact that Mattie never was seen reading her Bible or attending church services, especially since one of her brothers was a preacher. She also refused to join Carol and me in the room when we prayed. And I had a difficult time ignoring her negative actions and comments towards Carol, who seemed to not notice.

While we were at Washington, Mattie did not receive her GED, failing the needed score in Math by one point. I was very pleased to hear her say that she planned to have it before she went home to her children. And Carol and I encouraged her at every opportunity. When she decided to retake the Math portion of the GED, we were very proud of her. For several days leading up to the test, Carol and I secretly prayed for her to receive a passing score. On the day before the test, I told Mattie that Carol and I had been praying for her a passing score, the one point that she needed. I then asked her to join us in prayer. Mattie refused the invitation. She reminded me that she only needed one point to pass and said, "I can do that on my own, I don't need God for that." After that statement, it was several nights before I had a restful night's sleep. I was afraid of her!

Approximately two weeks after the test was taken, Mattie received her score. She had made the exact same score as before and again she failed, unable to score the one point that she needed. She did not need God and He did not need her. Mattie seemed devastated and could not believe what happened. But Carole and I kept on secretly praying. We absolutely refused to give up on her because we knew that God could do anything but fail.

Several weeks later, I asked Mattie if she was ready to take the test once more. She stated that she was never going to take the test again because obviously it was not meant for her to have her GED. She also said that she could not afford to pay the fee to take the test again. I told Mattie that what was obvious to Carol and me was that she could not pass the test all by her self. If she asked God to help her, He would do so. And because He was constantly blessing me, I blessed her by giving her the money to pay to take the test again. I also asked Sherry, who was a certified public accountant, to tutor Mattie and help prepare her for the test.

The very next time that Carol and I began to pray, we were thankful that Mattie joined us without an additional invitation. From that moment on, there was a special anointing in room 141. And we enjoyed spending time in our room together. Needless to say, Carol and I were not surprised when a couple of weeks later Mattie received a passing score. She had made the one point needed to earn her GED. And three days later, she learned her release date!

I knew that prayer was the key to keep all of us afloat. The night before Mattie was to be released from the transitional center, I planned a little "going away prayer meeting" in her honor. It was so successful that Carol asked me to please have one for her when it became time for her to leave the transitional center.

Our new roommate, Wanda Almond was a blessing. She had the same morning work schedule as Carol and me, and she fit in perfectly. It was a joy and an honor to join my two roommates in prayer as we started each new day. Satan did not stand a chance in room 141 because we stood united to defeat all negative attacks. We enjoyed each other's company.

Carol was disappointed and had her faith tested even more when she was not released during her scheduled month of October 2000. But we continued to pray, knowing that everything works according to God's plan for us... She knew that the delay in her release was somehow for her own good.

One day while at work, Cindy Johnson, one of my co-workers asked me if I had called "the computer" to see if my release date had been set. I had received some paperwork last year that said that I would be eligible for release December 2000. It was the middle of November and I told her "no," that I was trusting God for my release before Christmas and I was not going to be "jerked around by man" by listening to the computer.

Sheila Ferguson, also a co-worker, encouraged me to call saying that if anyone deserved to be released before Christmas, I did. My entire office had been extremely supportive throughout my employment and they wanted me to be free and home for the holidays.

Cindy asked for my "EF#" which is required whenever anyone is trying to get information concerning a release date from the Georgia Department of Corrections. I gave Cindy my number and found myself holding my breath. I was doing exactly what I said that I was not going to do, looking to man for my release. Cindy told me that the computer was saying my release would occur in December 2000. I was disappointed but in a strange way, relieved.

A couple of days after the initial call, I overheard Cindy talking on the phone. She said, "wait a minute, that is not what it said the last time I called." It is sounding like it is saying 12-4-00. I looked up from my work and said, "o.k. Cindy, I don't feel like joking around today. She said, "I am not joking, honest!"

Then I looked up at "Toi" another co-worker. She had been incarcerated at Washington State Prison and had been released the previous year. Toi said, "let me call the number." She placed a call to the computer, listened carefully and walked to my desk and gave me a hug. She said, "congratulations Ma, you'll be home for Christmas."

I went to the phone and again Cindy dialed the number for the computer. After entering my EF#, I listened to a voice say, this inmate is scheduled to be released on 12-4-00. I thanked God because He had heard my cry. I would be home, back in my house after 1,032 days, for the Christmas holidays.

On the bus ride from work, I made the decision that I would keep my release date from everyone except my family. I knew how difficult it had been for Carol to see others get a release date and go home when the computer said she should have been gone a month ago. So I decided that I would keep it from everyone and continue to support and encourage Carol.

When I reached the center one of the ladies shouted, "Mrs. Cash, good news, your bunkie got her date - November 30th! I was thrilled and very, very thankful. That night, Carol and I prayed together and thanked God for our deliverance. And we had a good night's sleep for the first time in a long, long time.

The night before her discharge from "The House," Carol's wish was granted. I informed the officer of our desire to gather in the classroom and have a "farewell prayer group" to strengthen Carol as she prepared to leave. Words designed to enhance, encourage, enrich, and empower were the best going away gifts available.

The officer announced over the intercom that Mrs. Cash was holding a group in the classroom and encouraged the other ladies to attend. When I arrived in the classroom, several of the ladies came thinking that I would be doing some kind of counseling. It was kind of funny to me because I realized that they actually thought I had authority that was not mine.

Carol was truly humbled by the positive remarks made by the ladies. She had no idea that the others were observing her Christian walk. Their words of encouragement were a source of inspiration for her as she prepared to leave "the nest." She was not ashamed to admit her fears about living back in the "free-world." Her ten years of addiction to crack cocaine and her career in prostitution would be a constant reminder of just how far God had brought her. Our prayers were that she would continue to trust God for everything that she needed.

On the morning that Carol was to leave "The House," I helped her to style her hair. I had already arranged for my girlfriend, Patricia Bowens, to pick her up and take her to "The Welcome House," the place that she was to parole out to. She had decided not to return to her hometown to live because of all the temptations that she would have to encounter, and she had no family in the Atlanta area. I did not want Carol to have to ride public transportation and struggle with all of her belongings and I would not be able to help because I would be at work. So my friend Patricia agreed to take Carol to her destination so that she would not have to struggle on the bus.

We prayed together and cried together. I made her promise to call me at work just as soon as she had arrived at her destination and settled down. I thanked God for bringing Carol into my life and asked Him to please keep a special eye on her!

That evening, Wanda and I got a new "Bunkie" but it just did not matter anymore. I had less than a week to remain at Metro Transitional Center before my release to return to my family and my home.

During my stay at "The House", the Chaplain had given me the name of a lady she wanted me to meet. This lady had a vision to open a Transitional Halfway House called SA'Mira's Place, a safe place for women being released from prison. The chaplain felt that I would be able to assist her, because of my background and previous contacts. Unfortunately we were unable to make contact with each other.

On the day before my last day at the center, I took an early evening nap and enjoyed a very peaceful dream. My mother was in the room with me and she had a very pleased smile on her face. She had visited me many times during my incarceration and while she had never said a word, I could tell that she was o.k. about "my assignment." This evening was no exception except she was lying on a bed next to mine reading a copy of <u>Comfortable Being Ignorant While Surviving the Journey</u> by JoAnn F. Cash. She appeared extremely pleased.

Just as I started to ask her what was she smiling about, there came a knock at the door and I woke up. The knock came from one of my closest friends at "The House" and my former neighbor in prison, Renee Lawrence. She asked me to come to the classroom in about twenty minutes.

After I washed my face and entered the classroom, I was stunned to see the number of ladies who had gathered to wish me farewell. They had the chairs formed in two lines facing each other and a chair in the middle of the room for "me". Each one talked about the lessons that they had learned and the impact that I had made on their lives. They all promised that this would be their very last time in prison. I just could not hold back the tears. I kept thinking, "they heard me!" All of my preaching and fussing had not been in vain.

Just after the program started, a lady entered the room and sat with the others. While she said nothing, she sat and observed the happenings. I later learned that this was Patricia "Trish" Lewis, the lady who the chaplain had wanted me to meet.

When the officer entered to tell us to go to our rooms for "count", one of the ladies stood up and said, "no" we ain't finished yet, so you need to go and get a count sheet and bring it back in here to us! I almost died. Interrupting "count" was a sure way to get sent back to prison. The officer left the room and returned a short time later with a count sheet for the ladies to sign so that we could continue with the program.

The following morning I began the day by thanking God for my deliverance. I knew that things were not going to be easy. There had been a lot of harm and damage done in my family and to my reputation. But I reminded God that His word said to ask, and He would give us the desires of our heart. I simply told Him that I wanted "everything" back that the devil had stolen from me, including my good name. I would definitely not stop until my appeal had been filed and my conviction overturned.

As I walked into the lobby to check out, there sat my husband and my son. One of the officers said, "come on freedom fighter." Another said, yes, I think she must be Sojourner Truth or somebody like that. Let's get her out of here. After I checked out, my family and I walked out the door. After 1,032 days of incarceration, my assignment had finally come to an end. As we reached the car, my family and I huddled for a brief prayer. I had survived the journey. As we drove away again, I thanked God!

What "Worth" The Journey

When trying to analyze the reasons for "my journey," I was totally at a lost as to the rationale for it. I would be the first person to say that I was not perfect, that my faults were numerous. But I always thought that, basically I was a good person, that I would reap what I had sown. I had always tried to be a good wife, a good mother, a good sister, and a good friend. I was raised to believe that if you did good things, then good things would happen to you. So, what's up with this!

In the midst of pondering my situation, I continued to hear the word "mother." I knew what motherhood was all about. Because of the example set by my mother, I knew of the major sacrifices and all of the caring and concern that was required in order to be a good one. And, to date, that was my biggest and proudest accomplishment.

I was very definite about what it took and what it meant to be a good mother. But while back in the Glynn County Detention Center, I found myself growing increasingly depressed about what I saw and heard with the daily interactions among the ladies. I found myself eaten up with bitterness listening to the conversations and watching the behaviors of my new friends and associates. It was impossible for me to forget that, first and foremost, ninety-eight percent of these ladies were mothers. Many days I resented having to be in their presence especially when I thought of the hurt and harm my absence had caused my family. Then something led me to see what <u>Webster's New World Dictionary</u> had to say about the actual meaning of the word.

Webster's definition of mother is defined (1.) As a female parent; (2) the origin or source of something. After reading that definition, I began to feel a little bit better about some of the ladies because I had a better understanding of them. Mother, for them, simply meant, "to be responsible for starting something, to bring life into being." Once life had been created, the job of motherhood had been completed. That helped me to understand how so many of them could give birth to a child and then leave them with "mama" to raise and nurture. That was all they knew to do because many of them had been raised by their grandparents. They simply continued the cycle due to their ignorance.

However, <u>The American Heritage Dictionary (Second College Edition)</u> offered a different definition for the same word. They defined mother as (1) a female parent, (2) a female who has a position of authority or responsibility similar to that of a mother; a housemother, (3) a creative source: origin, (4) an old or elderly woman, (5) to give birth to, to create produce, (6) to watch over, nourish and protect. And I was very much in agreement with their definition.

That is when I realized that I had committed a grave injustice. I had been very judgmental of these ladies when, in reality, they did not know any better. Their actions had been based, for the most part, on the information provided to them from people who thought they knew what they were talking about. They were just like me, comfortable being ignorant!

Now I had to face up to what I had done. And just who did I think I was? I had come into an environment with my own set of values and goals and truly expected to find the same thing. But when I did not, instead of trying to understand the reasons for the differences, I became judgmental and often drew my own conclusions.

I had spent a great deal of time questioning God as to why He had sent me on this journey. I knew that He did not make mistakes. So I decided to sit down and write out some benefits derived from this experience.

The first thing that I listed was the definition of the word mother. For the first time I truly realized that that word meant different things to different people. For some, their actions simply did not reflect their hearts.

And because of the seriousness of my beliefs as a mother, I now was afforded the opportunity to see just how overbearing and smothering I had been with my own son, Calvin. My absence allowed him an opportunity to be independent and grow up. And I could see the results of my labor. I did good!

I am sure that you have heard the saying, "behind every good man is a great woman." I was released from the position of being a "help-mate" to my husband and only had an actual responsibility for myself. I could focus on me.

One of my largest gains from this journey was my development for the love of reading. From my incarceration to my release, I read a total of one hundred and forty-five books.

This journey afforded me an opportunity to get a better understanding of the clientele served by Hand-in-Hand Counseling Services, Inc., and particularity those children whose mothers were away. I know now that much of their behavior was a smoke screen in their attempts to survive.

I was privileged to become friendly with an African American Psychiatrist who was also incarcerated at Washington State Prison. And we wrote, along with three other inmates as we walked the prison yard, a proposal, L.I.N.K. that means "Liaison for Inmates Needing Knowledge." There is a desperate need for an agency to foster communication between female inmates and the "free world."

My second greatest gain from this journey was learning to be tolerant and patient with others. I truly became less judgmental and more accepting of people for who they are. While no two of us are alike, we are all God's children.

Prior to this journey, it had been quite some time since I felt that I had to submit to anyone. I had had so much responsibility for so long. But this experience proved that I could be a "good" follower and not have to lead.

While my personal experiences with drugs had been limited, my journey helped me to learn respect and have a better understanding of addicts and their addictions.

Much too often we hear nothing but negative things about people who are incarcerated. But this journey afforded me an opportunity to meet some of the most beautiful people God created. Yes, there are some very nice and even some innocent people in prison.

This journey allowed me an opportunity to do what I do best, and that is work with others. I was instrumental, in my capacity as teacher's aide, to assist other ladies with writing their resumes and their study to obtain their G.E.D.

A major reward from this experience was documenting this information to be included in writing this book, <u>Comfortable Being Ignorant While Surviving the Journey.</u> In all probability, without this journey, I would have continued to believe that my life offered nothing to write about. This journey let me know, without a shadow of a doubt, that I was wrong.

And last but certainly not least, this journey gave me an opportunity to learn to lean and depend on Jesus. I now know what I am made of because I know that I have been chosen by Him to do a mighty work. I know that this battle is not mine but His. Truly our trials and tribulations are only a test of our faith. And I know that greater is He that is in me than he that is in the world.

After I realized that I was blessed and highly favored, I knew that it was necessary for me to change my way of thinking about some of the ladies that I had met. I had judged them falsely and a voice said, "we all have sinned and fallen short," it is time for you to forgive them. Then you will be ready to heal.

Approximately six weeks after I made my list of benefits from this journey, I was asked to speak to the March Kairos Reunion. The following is my speech that I delivered to about two hundred ladies at Washington State Prison:

When Audrey asked me to speak on a major change that had occurred in my life since my "Four Day Walk" at Kairos #7 at the table of Martha, immediately I flashed back and reminisced on just how the Forgiveness Ceremony had impacted my life. After deciding that I would attempt to speak on the subject of forgiveness, I decided that it was a good idea to first look up the definition.

According to the <u>American Heritage Dictionary</u>, forgiveness means (1) to excuse for a fault or offense, pardon, (2) to renounce anger or resentment against, (3) to absolve from payment, (4) to accord forgiveness.

The synonyms: forgive and excuse. These verbs mean to pass over an offense and to free the offender from the consequences of it. To forgive is to grant pardon without harboring resentment.

When I looked in the <u>Bible</u> about forgiveness, the <u>New International Version</u>, Matthew 5:7 says: "Blessed are the merciful; for they shall obtain mercy." Ephesians 4:32 says, "be ye kind one to another, tenderhearted, forgiving one another, even as God for Christ's sake hath forgiven you."

<u>The International Bible</u> in Matthew 5:44 says, but here is what I tell you. Love your enemies. Pray for those who hurt you.

<u>The Authorized King James Version</u> was the most healing for me. It said in Matthew 5:44- But I say unto you. Love your enemies, bless them that curse you, do good to them that hate you and pray for them which despitefully use you and persecute you.

It helped me to realize that I had actually forgiven two females that I thought I would despise for the rest of my life, the first two names I had listed on my forgiveness sheet and placed in the bowl to be dissolved…my judge, Wilma Anderson and the prosecutor, Niki Adams.

Not only was I unjustly prosecuted and sentenced but also in October, 1999 after being eligible for parole, these same two ladies opposed my release…because I had shown no remorse they continued with their personal interest in "teaching me a lesson."

On January 14, 2000, I again had an opportunity to face the same two ladies. The minute I saw them I began to pray for them. They looked terrible! Yes, they had sent me to prison but "free" they were in worst shape than me. I prayed and asked God to meet them at the point of their needs. And without Kairos and the forgiveness Ceremony, I would not have been able to do that!

On that same forgiveness paper, I also listed the names of my husband and my son. I was experiencing negative feeling towards them because they were going on with their lives without me. Prior to my incarceration we had never been separated and I had become convinced that they needed me and that they would not be able to "make it" without me. It hurt to find out that I was wrong. And I held it against them!

Deep down I was hurt when I heard about their day-to-day activities and I was not able to participate with them. I was hurt when they did not visit me on weekends. I was hurt when I would call home and they sounded happy, when I was so miserable. I hurt because they did not love me enough to stop living without me.

Kairos and the Forgiveness Ceremony changed my way of thinking. And because of their agape love, that God wants all of His children to have, I was able to forgive.

Now I count my blessings. I am blessed to have a husband of almost thirty years who has kept our household in tact during my absence. I am blessed that my almost twenty-three year old son, who works as a nationally certified pharmaceutical technician five days a week also works at another drug store on weekends to help out at home. In addition to this, he is attending his college classes three mornings a week working on a major in computer technology. Yes, I am talking about my son, an outstanding African American male, the kind that you seldom hear about! And he also sends money to his mother. I am truly blessed.

Although there were several other names on "the list of forgiveness," the last name I want to share with you was the name JoAnn F. Cash. Yes, I was in desperate need of forgiveness. I had become judgmental and resentful towards many of the mothers I had met during my incarceration. And I was mad at myself for caring about them and their children.

Many of these females had not placed their priorities on getting back home and being the responsible mother that their children deserved. It was incomprehensible to me that women would prefer to remain in prison with their "bull-dagger" than to return home to their children. I was hurt and disappointed at much of their attitudes and behavior, especially after having invested my professional career and adult life working with other people's children. Because of Hand-in-Hand Counseling Services' efforts to fill the gap in the lives of children caused by the absence of their mothers, either caused by drug addiction, jail or some other form of ineffective parenting, I find myself in prison!

I hated myself for caring more about some of the children than their mothers' cared. One of my major goals had been to re-unify mother and child, and in the process, I had become separated from mine. Yes, I was mad at them and I hated myself for the harm I had caused my family, putting other families before mine. I needed to forgive me!

While in the midst of my struggling and asking myself whether or not my efforts had been in vain, Kairos proved to me, at a time when I needed it most, that it is all about LOVE. I get great comfort in the Bible, The New International Version of I Corinthians 13:4-8: "love is patient, love is kind. It does not envy, it does not boast, it is not proud. It is not rude, it is not self-seeking, it is not easily angered, it keeps no record of wrongs. Love does not delight in evil but rejoices with the truth. It always protects, always trusts. Always hopes, always perseveres...Love never fails"

Kairos reminded me of the Love of God for all of us. He gave His only begotten son that we might live. Now that was the ultimate price! I saw that my feeble attempts at helping others were what, as a Christian, I was supposed to do. And knowing that, I was able to forgive.

My actions were not about me, but as Phyl Macon often reminded me, the God in me. I did no more than God would have me do. And He too suffered, especially in His hometown. And He, Paul and many other great men, Dr. Martin Luther King, Jr. included were sent to jail for doing good.

In looking back over my one thousand and thirty-two day journey, I know that God orchestrated my trip. He was there to show me favor every step of the way. When I could not walk, He carried me. I am convinced, without a shadow of doubt that I am one of the "chosen" children of God. And I know that I am blessed and highly favored.

I now know exactly why I was sent to prison. It was an attack of the enemy. But today as always, I continue to rebuke Satan. No, he cannot have me, nor can he have my family.

Just like Paul in Philippians 1:12-16 (Free on the Inside International Bible) "Brothers and sisters, here is what I want you to know. What has happened to me has helped to spread the good news. One thing has become clear. I am being held by chains because of my stand for Christ. All of the palace guards and everyone else know it. Because I am being held by chains, most of the believers in the LORD have become bolder. They now speak God's word more boldly and without fear. It's true that some preach about Christ because they are jealous. But others preach about Christ to help me in my work. The last group acts out of LOVE. They know I have been put here to stand up for the good news."

Letters from the Ladies Inside
Uncensored

11/4/00

How God send blessing in disguise

I met Mrs. Cash one day during the time that I was off and had a outside detail picking dandelions. The sun was hot that day, But that was the day we made up our minds that we were Sisters in Christ. She was still in the B Bldg. But when she moved to A Bldg., that's when I realized how remarkable this woman could be. She move in the room one day and rearrange where our shoes were position. Because she says that my shoes smell like smoke and she didn't think they had to be put under her head. That was just fine with me. But one morning before I went to work, we had a talk a very serious talk about my life and the life of my children how discourage I was that morning. But she explain some things that morning with tears in her eyes and I was enlightened in a new way to rebuild and reestablish the relationship with my children. I will be ever blessed by that day. And the day that Mrs. Joann Cash became my roommate. We will be forever sisters in Christ. I shall never forget this woman. Because as we touch and agree in prayer, I know God has delivered us both and will deliver us from these circumstances also. I will always be grateful for any free counseling that I have receive and will receive. But I am also willing to pay a small fee.

Love You
Carol
10/31/00

WHAT MEETING JOANNE CASH MEANT TO ME

Let me say right now, that Mrs. Cash is a God sent person. She has the heart, and soul of an angel. I first met Mrs. Cash at Washington State Prison, she was my G-sams teacher aide. She encourage me every day not to give up, even when I felt like I was the dumbest person in class. Thanks to Mrs. Joanne Cash, I received my G.E.D. on October 6th 2000. Not only has Mrs. Cash been there for me, but also all of the other ladies here at M.T.C. has benefitted from Mrs. Cash wisdom. You can't go hungry, or without clothing with Mrs. Cash around. I have seen her a many times give her own food to someone hungry, and literarily given the shirt off her back to someone who needed clothing. It was my honor to meet Mrs. Joanne Cash, and my life, and all who has met her has been inspired.

P.S. God Bless You Mrs. Joanne Cash
I Love You   Mattie T.

138

Some people can spend a lifetime not knowing their purpose. But it's an awesome experience to come in contact with someone who recognizes and submits to Christ Jesus as the lady I call my Guardian Angel, Mrs. Cash. I will never forget the day I met her how empty and alone I was feeling and the way she detected those feelings and did not hesitate when she was called to my rescue her words to me were "child everything you are feeling is only a test she was so patient at explaining to me to not allow my situation to feed negativity utilize each day to the fullest as a journey of learning experiences and to not fear these things when chosen by God these things we can and will do "I felt so much strength instantly the weights were lifted and I gained some direction far from perfect yet I understand months later I ran across her again when I spoke and reminded her of that conversation she was in complete awe as I explained to her the impact she made on my life. I can never thank God enough for her obedience in guiding a stray shepherd and to her I dedicate these words with true and sincere Sisterly Love.

Vanessa H.

My name is Brenda, I'm 33 years, and I have three children. I love Mother Cash like a real daughter would love her own mother. To put her into words would be more than a mouth full. First I would say she's a Godly blessed woman of God, inspirational, and true friend.

The first time I heard her name there were saying she thinks she all that. I didn't know her then. What was running through my mind was if there making all this fuss about one woman then its got to something special about her. I watched her and what I saw was giving to the needy when she could, her doing bible studies, and willingness to help others. She even gotten into some jams while helping somebody else because she saw the need. I decided she was good for me. Sometimes I would go sit with her and could feel the presence of God around her. My birth mother is deceased but some reason it was easy to call Mother. I respect her to the fullest. She's never to busy for me. I get a little mad at these new girls coming in trying to be family. Myself and one of Mother Cash other daughters had a girl hemmed up on the yard. Mother Cash made us leave her alone. I had to remind myself that she is doing what she do best loving and caring for others. I really love my Mother and beyond this place we may go separate ways she will always be my Mother and I will always be there for her. When I think about her I think GREATNESS.

On this journey of incarceration, I was blessed and fortunate to travel with a woman who is so very REAL and who lives and walks as a Child of

God—a true Christian. Joanne Cash is this woman and I have learned that she is capable of Relating to men and women of all nationalities, backgrounds and positions. This woman can communicate with the very elite or someone of low economic standards.

She's Energetic and always ready to take on the challenge in spite of age. She's Alert to her surroundings and can discern when and where there is a need with an individual or with any situation. And finally, she is a Loving and caring person. There isn't a day that goes by that genuine love and concern hasn't touched someone. Her words of encouragement will simply lighten the load of any weary traveler. Who wouldn" want to befriend or come in contact with a courageous and innovative, fun loving and full of energy woman such as Joanne Cash. Our meeting truly was by divine appointment from God Almighty even under these adverse conditions.

Mrs. Cash deserves the best God has in store for her. May everything she touches prosper and comes to success.

Thanks Mrs. Cash for motivating my life. It was more than worth the journey.

Renee L.
Your Friend In Christ

"I Found a Friend"

Mrs. Cash,

I would like to tell you what you've meant to me since our stay at Metro Transitional Center. When I think about how we first met, I'll have to smile, because I thought you were the meanest lady I'd ever met, because of something that I wanted on my tray at dinner in the dining Hall, and you said "No" due to the rules and that I would have to wait until seconds were called, so I told my friend "quote that Mrs. Cash lady is mean and I hope I never have to deal with her again end quote." Then the very next week they put me in the room with guess who? Right, MRS. CASH. And I just knew this wasn't going to work out, but let me just say that Satan is a liar and I found not only a true Christian lady, but also a true friend. A person that is just as sweet on the inside as the outside. A person who is willing to help in any way she can and always carries others in her heart and prayers. You Mrs. Cash, has been my rock in this hard place. My friend when I was friendless. My Mother when I was Motherless. My doctor when I was sick.

Mrs. Cash you've prayed for me and I thank God for putting you right where you were needed most, because if it hadn't been for you I truly don't think I would have made it and remember this; God put people in the places they need to be and M.T.C. was yours because so many ladies like myself needed someone to reach out they're hands and say I am here if you need a friend and that you've truly been to me and I know in my heart that you must rest so good at night because, you have touched so many ladies in this prison system in so many different ways to help them walk out of these revolving doors. But if they take what you have given them, as I will, then these doors will never have to revolve around them again. Your key words are...If you make God the head of your life then everything else will fall in place. Now last but not least, I believe God is smiling down on you saying, <u>Job Well Done My Child</u>. And I'm truly honored to say that I'm also proud of you, too. Thanks and may God's Blessing never stop pouring down on you, because you deserve nothing but the BEST.

Love Always,
Lisa J.

4/1/01

When I (Bobbie C.) met Mrs. Cash it was 1999 at Washington State Prison. I know now that God allowed her to be here to help women like me. Mrs. Cash and I were roommates or as we call them bunkies. We were going through P.S.A.P. (Prison Substance Abuse Program). Not that Mrs. Cash needed the program. But God used her in a mighty way, because she was obedient. At first I didn't understand. But as time passed I realized I could talk to Mrs. Cash and not only did she listen, she really cared. Even though we were going through a lot Mrs. Cash used patience and grace to help me and a lot of the other ladies. It was like a family bond between us. Not all of us but the majority. Mrs. Cash went out of her way to feed those that didn't have, to speak a word when it was really needed, and she never looked down on others because of what she had. She was generous and down to earth. The one thing I will always remember is how she told me how to allow God to heal me. Mrs. Cash and I ate soups together. The food here isn't that good. And I remember the time I brought back some food from the dining hall and Mrs. Cash got scared because we weren't supposed to do that. Mrs. Cash would not do anything wrong, to go against the rules, but feed you. Mrs. Cash taught me how to change my way of thinking. We prayed together for our family. She taught me how to do time and not let time do me. Mrs. Cash showed love daily and she helped me to do the same. I have a big mouth and I have a tendency to talk to much. And I am short. Mrs. Cash was always telling the ladies that I was sorry and she kept me from getting beat up. She allowed me to see how words hurt. And to hold my head up high. We went to her when we had a problem. The staff members here loved her also. Like Jesus, once you meet Mrs. Cash your life is never the same.

God Bless You Always,
Bobbie C.